why argument matters

yale

university

press

new haven

and

london

lee

siegel

why

argument

matters

168

Yale University Press books may be purchased in quantity for educational, business, or promotional use. For information, please e-mail sales.press@yale.edu (U.S. office) or sales@yaleup.co.uk (U.K. office).

Set in Adobe Garamond type by IDS Infotech Ltd. Printed in the United States of America.

Library of Congress Control Number: 2021941205
ISBN 978-0-300-24426-7 (hardcover : alk. paper)
A catalogue record for this book is available from the British Library.

This paper meets the requirements of ANSI/NISO Z39.48-1992 (Permanence of Paper).

10 9 8 7 6 5 4 3 2 1

also by lee siegel

Falling Upwards: Essays in Defense of the Imagination
Not Remotely Controlled: Notes on Television
Against the Machine: Being Human in the Age of
  the Electronic Mob
Are You Serious? How to Be True and Get Real in
  the Age of Silly
Groucho Marx: The Comedy of Existence
The Draw: A Memoir

For Julian and Harper

contents

why argument matters

prologue

Many useful books have been written about how to win an argument—in court, in school, at work and at play, in a retail situation, in a parking lot kerfuffle, in the bedroom, in 280 characters. What all these different types of disagreement have in common is that they are transactional: an exchange of words results in either gain or loss. This book, however, aims to offer a practical usefulness based on a higher aspiration. It is about argument's roots in our very existence, argument that is as natural and inevitable a condition of our being as breathing: *Dum spiro arguo.* I am interested in argument as the expression of a universal longing for a better life.

Though I will certainly encompass arguments that occur between adversaries, the arguments that I have in mind are not wranglings over one position or another. They are justifications for ways of living. Such arguments do not require the presence of an opponent. The "adversary" on these occasions is not a person but a social, cultural, or political condition. The most powerful and memorable arguments are made in a speech, a treatise, an essay, a critique—Martin Luther King's "I Have a Dream" speech, Edmund Burke's *Vindication of Natural Society,* René Descartes's *Discourse on Method,* George Orwell's "Politics and the English Language," Virginia Woolf's *A Room of One's Own.* These make argument, contrary to the popular conception of it as a gregarious undertaking, the product of solitude, like art, or like any type of profound contemplation. It is my hope that part of this book's usefulness will be to add another resource to the reader's solitude.

The book's first part, "The Art of Argument," explores argument as a categorical challenge to the status quo that seeks to modify, amplify, or replace one set of givens with another. Here argument can appeal to the emotions, it can employ subtlety and nuance, but it is always a categorical statement about existence. Its most powerful tactic, however, has little to do with logic and rhetoric.

A true argument depends upon two qualities: an intense concern for the matter at hand that extends beyond merely winning or losing the argument, and the ability to live the thoughts and emotions behind the counterargument. The most relentless, intellectually merciless arguments are acts of caring about the world—again, persuasion as the vision of a better life—with a grasp of your opponent's inwardness as the instrument of mastery.

Such imaginative inhabitation of an opponent has two purposes. One is to know your opponent's mind the more completely to dismantle—or discredit, or even destroy—his* argument. The other is to know your opponent's mind in order to join with him in a common humanity, regardless of the argument's outcome. And in the event that the sincere embodiment of a common humanity within the structure of an argument helps you to carry the day, then so much the better.

The second part of the book, "The Argument of Art," explores art as an argument for the dignity of human existence itself. If a work of art, by getting closer to what is real, can reproduce human existence in all its multiplicity of truth, then art proves that life can be created out of the imagination just as surely as out of a biological cell. A successful work of art makes the argument that humanity can transcend its material conditions.

* In order to avoid the linguistic eyesore of constantly repeating both the masculine and the feminine singular forms of the third-person pronoun, I have used the masculine form as a generic pronoun where necessary. I expect that a female or a nonbinary author would feel similarly justified in using the feminine singular or the third-person-plural pronoun as the generic form.

To put it another way, argument seeks to make one approach to life prevail over another for the sake of a larger and freer existence; art strives to convince us of the multifaceted nature of existence for the sake of a larger and freer argument. Like Penelope besieged by the suitors, truth is as wily as it is contested.

Let us be clear about what true argument, the art of argument, is not. It is not a quarrel. It is not a dispute. It is not a debate. Although I will sometimes use these words in place of "argument" for the sake of variation, elegant or otherwise, "argument" possesses a different meaning.

A quarrel is a disagreement inflamed by the ego.

A dispute is a disagreement restrained by the law.

A debate is a disagreement organized by the spirit of play.

A quarrel serves no purpose. It is set in motion when an individual's aggrieved self-interest runs up against another individual's aggrieved self-interest. Like those perpetually swinging metal balls known as "Newton's cradle" that used to adorn the desks of male business executives before the metaphorical image of colliding testicles lost its masculine allure, quarrels never end because the ego never rests.

No logic, evidence, or language will convince either my wife or me that it is the other's turn to unload the dishwasher this morning. Lacking the qualities of logic, evidence, and language, an argument cannot take place. A quarrel is an attempt to reposition the ego within the acreage created and shared by two or more egos. Since the acreage is a psychic abstraction, a quarrel does not follow rational lines.

A dispute contests impersonal boundaries. If my neighbor has just spent thousands of dollars on a new set of backyard LED lights and I complain that the lights are shining through my bedroom window, each of us will make a mental estimation of our legal rights.

Now should the quarrel between my wife and me about emptying the dishwasher lead to the process of divorce, then the quarrel would become a dispute, and the law would decide who gets our nice European dishwasher.

And if my neighbor and I decide that one of us has been not just unfairly imposed upon but personally insulted, then what should have been a dispute will simmer and seethe into a quarrel—unless we avoid interacting with each other. A quarrel requires a travesty of intimacy to be maintained.

A debate is free from the anger of a quarrel and from the looming process of a dispute. However, its freedom from feeling or formal redress makes it seek its own structure. A debate is a detached ritual of disagreement.

Though often used interchangeably with these other terms, a true argument stands apart from them.

Argument flows from our intuitive certainty that our right to exist is the most elemental truth, and that our right to exist is bound up with our freedom to think about existence in specific ways. These are abstractions that we hope will become real, either through subtlety and irony or through earnest declamation and attack. Argument is hope, sometimes at the chessboard and sometimes in the boxing ring.

Most examinations of argument, either from a practical or a theoretical perspective, begin with Aristotle, who defines rhetoric as "the power to see, in each case, the possible ways to persuade." From the outset, he identifies effective writing and speaking with persuasion: that is, argument.

This fairly innocent definition of argument is often the starting point for the presentation of the "good" Aristotle, the Aristotle of advanced-placement high school classes and the required college freshman composition course. This nice, helpful Aristotle will easily get students through their sophomore year if they learn his basic precepts of rhetoric.

In the "good" Aristotle, you've got your ethos—the credibility, character, or status of the speaker; your pathos—the reader or listener's emotional condition; and your logos—the linguistic and logical properties of the argument itself. Aristotle's three principles are often applied in later careers within various spheres, realms of life that Aristotle also instructively lays out. They are the "deliberative," which Aristotle defines as a political speech before a parliamentary assembly, but which applies to any address made to a group—an academic committee meeting, the board of one organization of another, the local PTA. The "judicial" is a court of law. The "epideictic," a ceremonial speech, seems particularly relevant to our otherwise unceremonial time. It levels blame or confers praise, using as its central means of persuasion a characterization of its target's behavior as dishonorable or shameful.

That last category hints at the "bad," or dark, Aristotle, who is something else again. Part of Aristotle's motive in writing the *Rhetoric* was to refute charges made by Plato and Aristophanes that rhetoric enables injustice and obscures truth. "Arguments, like men, are often pretenders," wrote Plato, the thwarted playwright. For Aristotle, rhetoric, executed properly, ensures a harmony among all the disparate tensions of a democracy. In practice, though, his *Rhetoric* reads in places like a handbook for demagogues.

Aristotle fascinatingly lays out one strategy after another for playing on everything from people's feelings to their character to their situation in life: "Of the bodily desires, it is the sexual by which [the young] are most swayed"; the elderly "are small-minded because they have been humbled by life: their desires are set upon nothing more exalted or unusual than what will help them to keep alive"; "wealthy men are insolent and arrogant; their possession of wealth affects their understanding; they feel as if they had every good thing that exists; wealth becomes a sort of standard for everything else." He ranges far and wide in a treatise on the art of persuasion, exploring emotions such as envy, anger, and shame in his examination of the extent of argument's reach into human depths.

Aristotle prized language and logic, but he would have had in mind Pericles' Funeral Oration, celebrated as the very model of persuasion for centuries after it was delivered. After cleverly saying that the dead Athenian soldiers he has been asked to commemorate in words deserve to be hallowed by actions, this man of action declares that "it is difficult to say neither too little nor too much; and even moderation is apt not to give the impression of truthfulness."

Even moderation, says Pericles, can deceive! Moderation, the "golden mean," was the apple of Aristotle's philosophical eye. Pericles, so identified with the golden age of Athenian culture, in fact denigrates culture in favor of action, specifically military action. Indeed, it was Pericles' pursuit of war against Sparta that led to the downfall of Athens, as Aristotle well knew. The Funeral Oration's jingoism and censure of those who seek peace demonstrates both the inadequacy of words in the face of action and the power of words to create action. No wonder Aristotle, in his analysis of the art of persuasion, looked for verbal strategies that went straight to the core of the psyche, verbal strategies that were nearly as effective as action.

For Aristotle, then, the effective arguer knows how to manipulate an audience by adjusting an argument to the audience's psychological weaknesses and needs. This is not simply the stuff of demagoguery. It also drives commercial strategies for relieving people of their money. Business people and bankers have Sun Tzu on their office bookshelves; public relations strategists and marketing people put a few pensées from Aristotle on their websites.

Before Aristotle, Socrates had dismissed the art of argument as not just deleterious to the health of a republic but, almost equally harmful in his eyes, as a type of "cooking," devoted merely to "the production of gratification and pleasure." Still, as Socrates the pioneering dialectician knew well, argument at its eloquent, rational, impassioned best is hardly sordid, and hardly less essential to a republic than Socrates' own style of ironic probing for the truth. Aristotle was getting at the heart of human existence when he identified rhetoric solely as the art of persuasion and made that art encompass the human condition. The following pages will cover arguments high, low, and all degrees in between.

This book's chief aspiration, though, will be to treat argument, or, rather, to uncover argument as Socrates ultimately practiced it. I don't mean his famous dialectical method, which is as much cross-examination as it was, at the time, a new type of argument. At the end of his life, Socrates stripped argument down to its essence as a type of transcendent fusion of language, meaning, feeling, and action.

You may recall that Socrates, having been convicted of "impiety" and "corrupting the young," told a friend that he was choosing to drink the lethal hemlock in order to comply with his death sentence instead of taking up his friend's offer to flee Athens. Since he had lived under Athenian law, Socrates explained, he was obligated to die under it. But it is hard to believe that Socrates, who had devoted his life to a rational search for the truth, would make his death the validation of a verdict on him that was neither rational nor true.

What he was really doing, it seems to me, was enacting his own "Socratic" irony in the profoundest sense. By declaring that he was killing himself in accordance with the law, he was demonstrating that a law that would order a true philosopher to kill himself was inhuman and unjust. Socrates' final act was to make argument indistinguishable from human existence.

He made his willingness to die for the truth proof of his argument for the necessity of *searching* for the truth.

To put it a little more light-heartedly, this book will be an account of argument that will also *be* an argument. Otherwise it would be about as exciting as a bird writing a monograph on ornithology. You have to be swept up into a thing to give a full account of it.

introduction

Especially lately, commentators have indulged in a kind of rueful sentimentality about the nature of argument. Individuals used to engage in high-minded debates, the lament goes, whereas now all they do is yell at each other or allow measured argument to decline into insult and personal attacks.

Yet people proverbially counseled against arguing about either politics or religion long before social media turned raging about both into a narcotic pleasure. It is nearly impossible to have a rational argument about political or religious beliefs that have been, almost by definition, arrived at along irrational psychic paths.

It is nearly impossible to have a rational argument that is not built out of the sticks and stones of emotion, period. Written in 55 BCE, Cicero's *De oratore* is a classic treatise on how to argue, though in places it might sound to contemporary ears like a description of how far argument has declined from the popular conception of its orderly classical proportions: "Now nothing in oratory . . . is more important than to win for the orator the favor of his hearer, and to have the latter so affected as to be swayed by something resembling a mental impulse or emotion, rather than by judgment or deliberation. For men decide far more problems by hate, or love, or lust, or rage, or sorrow, or joy, or hope, or fear, or illusion, or some other inward emotion, than by reality, or authority, or any legal standard, or judicial precedent, or statute." Contrast this with Barack Obama lamenting in his presidential memoir that while in the White House he came to realize that "whether I liked it or not, people were moved by emotion, not facts." This is an idealized understanding of the role of feeling in argument.

As for those Apollonian days of calm, rational, public debate: Caesar was murdered, not debated, that March day on the floor of the Roman Senate. In 1856, a pro-slavery member of the House of Representatives strode into the Senate chamber and caned the anti-slavery Republican senator from Massachusetts, Charles Sumner, nearly to death. In the British Parliament, jeers and booing are common from the back bench, and although an elegant riposte has often clinched an argument, gross insults sometimes erupt. Then–Prime Minister Margaret Thatcher was called a "sex-starved boa constrictor" on the floor of Parliament, a cut upon which any Twitter troll would cast a longing eye.

Emotionally charged manipulations of the truth were present in our hallowed deliberative halls before Twitter. Covering the Senate confirmation hearings for Justice Samuel Alito in January 2006, I ran, along with a gaggle of journalists, after Alito's wife, Martha-Ann Bomgardner, when she fled the chamber seemingly in tears following an aggressive question about her husband's stance on abortion. When I reached her after she stopped running, standing a few inches away from her, I watched as she removed her hands from her face. Not only were her eyes dry, she was smiling. The theatrical scene had the desired effect of derailing an argument in progress.

Argument is as Dionysian as it is Apollonian. It is ironic that many of the same people who decry the disappearance of calm, rational debate enthusiastically assent to the theories of the Israeli psychologists Daniel Kahneman and Amos Tversky, who posited, in highly influential academic papers they published throughout the 1980s, that the myriad ways in which reality is irrationally "framed" influence how we interpret reality—which is another way of saying that an argument is too influenced by extraneous factors to be rational. The choice of a word, the inclusion or omission of a detail, an inflection of sincerity or irony, the tone of a voice can determine our response to even the most critical decisions we must make in the course of our lives.

However, the opportunities for the application of a cognitive frame are nearly limitless.

FRAME ONE: Argument explodes the artifice of "framing" by its conscious transformation of social manipulation into formal persuasion.

FRAME TWO: Argument restores free will to human affairs by replacing the reductionist premises of Kahneman and Tversky with a process of transparent rational deliberation.

FRAME THREE: The concept of framing assumes that people don't recognize when reality is being framed. Therefore the concept of framing itself is the product of a narrowly framed understanding of human nature.

In other words, you could even frame the concept of framing to make one type of argument or another. Argument lives as a rational, as well as an emotional, activity, after all.

Social dynamics may be saturated with subtle modes of argumentation, but argument is in our flesh and blood.

In *Mysticism,* her classic study on the subject, the Anglo-Catholic writer Evelyn Underhill writes that the "beginning, for human thought, is of course the I, the Ego . . . which declares, in the teeth of all arguments, I AM." She adds, "The uncertainties only begin for most of us when we ask what else is." Yet for all of us, we begin asking what else is as soon as we are able to speak. And from Descartes on, even the formal structures of philosophical thought have been dedicated to demonstrating that we cannot prove that we ourselves exist. In such a situation, where argument is woven into biological existence itself, a beautifully constructed argument possesses the ragged contours of human life.

Bound up with the urgency of living, argument is as much an autobiographical process as it is an intellectual construction and a rhetorical art. Because our very life is an ongoing argument about the value of our life, the way we argue tells a story about who we are.

Take the philosopher Spinoza. As the child of Dutch Marranos who was later excommunicated by the Dutch Jewish community for, among other things, his attraction to Christian ideas, Spinoza lived out a divided nature. Born Baruch Spinoza, he changed his first name to Benedict after his expulsion. No wonder he refused to accept Descartes's segregation of mind from body, arguing instead for a picture of reality in which God's pantheistic presence provided a bridge between the two. And no wonder that he was the only philosopher to explicitly use Euclid's geometrical method in making his arguments in his *Ethics.* The geometrical method gave explicit expression to the two sides of his nature—Jewish and logical, Christian and abstract—while also providing an intellectual resolution to his rivenness.

In *Against Interpretation,* her seminal essay making a case that the meaning of art lies not in the imposition of any kind of stable, articulable meaning, Susan Sontag argues that a work of art is indistinguishable from its form. Thus a work of art cannot be captured or classified. Sontag herself was "queer" before that became a defining, or undefining, social term. Like the thesis of her argument, her sexuality could not be captured or classified.

Consider the lilies of the field, how they grow; they toil not, neither do they spin. But give two lilies the double-edged blessing of consciousness, and within minutes they will be arguing with each other. And each lily's argument will be the expression of its unique, particular existence. This fact of disputation being as primal as what Christians call original sin is what the French Catholic writer Charles Péguy meant when he said that "everything begins in mystery, and ends in politics."

Years ago, the *New Yorker* magazine ran a cartoon that depicted a grid composed of small squares extending infinitely in all directions. Each square was occupied by a person. There were no empty squares beyond the square that each person stood on. In the front row, one man is turning to the man standing next to him and saying, "Excuse me, sir. I am prepared to make you a rather attractive offer for your square." To exist is to argue your existence.

Familiar types of argument come to mind: the forceful speech, the mordant polemic, the debater pressing a point with a breathtaking flourish, the carefully staged summation to a jury. These are the forms argument takes as a consciously practiced art. But simply occupying a space in the world as a human being is an argument with a society that needs to know we exist.

"Attention must be paid!" cries Willy Loman's widow at the end of Arthur Miller's *Death of a Salesman.* No matter what place we occupy in life, there are moments when we have to make the same argument on our, or someone else's, behalf—to a spouse, a lover, a friend, a colleague, a business connection, a doctor, a cop, a judge, a neighbor, a stranger turned adversary by a sudden change of circumstance. "I know my own heart and thus I understand all humankind," postulated Jean-Jacques Rousseau at the beginning of his *Confessions,* one in a long line of autobiographies, from Saint Augustine's to Ta-Nehisi Coates's, that demonstrate how a particular life is really an argument for that particular life.

"Hineni," say Moses and Abraham when Yahweh asks, "Where are you?" They are not saying, "I am here," but rather "I am in this moral position in life where I am ready and willing to do your bidding." In everyday life, the response to a divine being asking such an existential question would be an argument. The response might be "I am not ready for this, and this is why" or, as Gloria Gaynor sang in another context, in another argument, "I'm not that chained-up little person still in love with you." Or the call might cause a different argument: "I have to leave my obligation to you because God is calling me and this is why I have to obey the call."

"Hier stehe ich," proclaimed Martin Luther, "Here I stand," thus turning the richly ambiguous "Here am I" into a defiant Protestant argument that has raged, intellectually and also bloodily, for centuries. We all say, or refuse to say, "Here am I" or "Here I stand," in one way or another, every minute of our lives. Then we argue for or against the consequences.

"That it was suddenly and obviously there, a person not from another town or from a different country but from life itself, the simplicity of that, was communicating to him a clarity and precision of purpose" is how the novelist Ian McEwan describes the effect that witnessing the birth of a child has on its father. The child is the subject of an argument the parent will make on its behalf to all the world, ceaselessly. With its appearance, the child begins its own argument. A child is born. Space is made. Attention is drawn. Water and oxygen are consumed. Matter is appropriated and evacuated. The entire world readjusts itself, if imperceptibly, microscopically. As the child's purpose becomes clear, as its appetites grow, as its personality declares ambitions and imposes boundaries, as the world yields or resists or simply bides its time, an argument is being made— on both sides.

"Son" begins Ta-Nehisi Coates's memoir *Between the World and Me,* addressed to his little boy. What more definite and defiant way to start an autobiographical polemic?

Or to come at it from the opposite direction: as Joseph Conrad put it in *Nostromo,* whenever someone dies, that person's particular truth leaves the world. Nothing presented as truth has ever gone uncontested. Neither has any human life.

"Let there be light" are Yahweh's first words in the Bible, spoken with luxuriant ease in absolute isolation. Only a transcendent being, existing outside time and space, history and society, can speak in declarative sentences that are as uncontested as such a being's existence would be. Introduce even a single human consciousness, and argument is sure to follow.

The authors of the Hebrew Bible made argument as primal and elemental as the Garden of Eden. They were keenly aware of the complicated status of argument as something good or bad, as a corrective of overweening power or an instrument of power itself. The first words spoken by a human being in the Bible belong to Eve, in response to the serpent, who has cunningly asked her if God really told her not to eat of any tree in the garden, thus implying that God is treating her and Adam unfairly.

Eve answers, "We may eat fruit from the trees in the garden, but God did say, 'You must not eat fruit from the tree that is in the middle of the garden, and you must not touch it, or you will die' " (Genesis 3:2–3). By quoting God's prohibition instead of paraphrasing it, as she does the other part of his instructions, she is inviting the serpent to offer his own interpretation of God's words, and his own advice about how to respond to them, perhaps hoping that he will justify her sense of being mistreated. That is to say, Eve is starting an argument with God by stripping his words of their luxuriant ease and making them as contingent on context as all mortal words are. Eve's first words, the first words of newly created humanity, are the beginning of an argument.

They are also a revelation of the power that argument has to transform an imbalance of power. Since what is good and what is bad are usually matters of interpretation, what God's prohibition foreclosed was a situation in which the human beings he created would argue with him, a situation in which he would not be able to say "let there be" anything without a debate.

Finally, this subtle argument with God that Eve is starting is the Bible authors' own argument. It is not rhetorical, though; it is poetic. We shall examine the argument of poetry, of art, in part II. But this instance is too good, and too instructive, to let pass.

After eating from the forbidden tree, Adam and Eve hear God "walking in the garden in the cool of the day," and then hide from him. But why would God be walking in the garden precisely at the moment when it becomes cool? The provocative implication is that God was waiting until the cool of the evening to take his walk because like any mortal he wanted to avoid the heat. God's own creation was beginning to bedevil him, and that creation includes Adam and Eve. This lovely realistic detail was perhaps the authors' argument that divinity itself was human and that therefore humans shared in the nature of the divine. It was an argument that would continue through painters' depictions of Christ that demonstrated Christ's humanity in the expression of his face or even the portrayal of the Christ Child's phallus.

Now a skeptic could respond to my argument by saying this is all nonsense. First of all, such a skeptic might argue, I am using the King James translation here. The Hebrew word translated as "cool of day," or sometimes as "breezy," could well derive from an Akkadian word meaning "storm." This would have God walking in "the wind of the storm," a rendering that is appropriate since Adam and Eve fear his wrath for having disobeyed him. Still others could dismiss my interpretation as both labored and tendentious. The breathtaking, realistic touch is no more than that, the biblical authors having fun by inserting a mundane detail from life into the sublime setting.

May the best side win.

Argument goes so far back because argument is, you might say, an ontological necessity.

A standard definition of ontology is (in part): an effort to prove that what seems to be an abstraction actually exists. Your spouse or partner argues with you about your habit of leaving crumbs on the kitchen table after lunch because she or he is trying to make the idea of a clean and tidy house a reality. And if that argument actually hides a deeper argument between the two of you about your relationship, then you are both struggling to make suppressed desires real.

Lawyers in a courtroom, two neighbors each of whom feels wronged by the other, corporate board members, presidential advisors, participants in the monthly Board of Education meeting, drivers backing up into each other in a parking lot, the tradesperson who is feeling abused, the homeowner who is feeling cheated—each party has a concrete goal in mind at the end of the argument.

With the exception of lawyers in the courtroom, these situations might never rise to the level of argument, of course. Some might remain quarrels that never rise to the level of a dispute. Argument relies on logic, rhetoric, evidence, artful self-presentation. Two people shouting at each other in a supermarket is no more an argument than reaching across the board and grabbing your opponent's king in a game of chess. Shouting is usually the product of an ontological error. Your absolute certainty that you are right blots out the existence of the other person. War is not, as the bromide goes, the continuation of politics by other means. War is the conviction that a cause is too good, or too desperate, for the empathetic—in the sense that you must inhabit your opponent to understand your opponent—art of politics.

The almost proverbial shout- and screamfest that the internet has become is the product of this conviction that other people do not exist. It is the consequence of a technology that reduces other people to pliable, Gumby-like figments of the imagination. In terms of argument, the internet is one of the grossest ontological errors of our time. An argument conducted in words—as we shall see, arguments can also be made in pictures, music, and verse—has to be not just the sharpest rebuttal of an opponent's position. It has to be the fullest understanding of an opponent's position.

Argument lies at the heart of the human imagination, so it is not surprising that in the realm of religion argument is central. Argument can either validate the tenets of a religion or pose a grave threat to it. It is never far from the minds of religious scholars and authorities.

The Qur'an says, warily, "Man has ever been, most of anything, prone to dispute." Islamic scholars list several types of argument, ranging from the rich and productive to the petty, destructive, and impoverished. A commendable argument proves the truth by means of evidence. Discreditable arguments come in several forms: "Dispute to conceal the Truth"; "Dispute to show one's merit and belittle others"; "Dispute that causes enmity"; "Dispute that usurps the rights of others." It is significant that, for the most part, dispute leads to trouble. According to the Qur'an the Prophet Muhammad said, "I guarantee a house on the outskirts of Paradise for one who abandons arguments even if he is right."

Hinduism recognizes three different types of argument: Vada, Jalpa, and Vitanda. The most respected arguments—

Vada—rely on the practitioners' honesty and openness about their aim, and how well they employ the art of argument, maintain decorum, and show respect for the opponent. But these are not the types of arguments the architects of Hinduism focused on. They were more interested in the manifold actuality of argument.

Vada in fact is not really an argument. Rather, it is an amiable conversation between two parties who are not committed to making their point of view prevail. Vada becomes possible only when there are "two persons of equal merit and standing." Think of two mothers putting their heads together to resolve a conflict between their young daughters in pre-K. Vada is the ongoing, careful negotiation we make with reality every day of our lives, a gentle persuasion that never rises to the level of argument.

Jalpa and Vitanda, by contrast, are arguments. They are made with the goal of winning, and neither one sticks to the intellectual or behavioral decorum of debate. The aim of the first is to use any rhetorical means necessary to demolish the opponent's position—no full understanding of the opponent's position here. The second also aims for absolute victory, but in addition, the arguer strives to shame and humiliate the opponent. A literary editor once told me why he was particularly proud of a polemical book review he had written years before. "I called X's book 'weak but important,' " he said. "Ah," he added with a satisfied smile, "that 'weak' really got to him." That is Vitanda.

In politics, in screen-dominated social life, Vitanda seems to have almost entirely displaced rational argument. One reason for this development is that in the West, at least, a long process of unmasking—in academia, in the media, in popular culture— has now led to a general belief that behind all the forms of law, custom, and civility stands the naked lust for power.

It sometimes seems that who gets to say what on which platform makes power, status, and authority more naked issues than ever before. But the truth is that imbalances of power have always been tangled up in the sources of arguments major and minor. Socrates, for example, invented his method to discredit the socially powerful Sophists. The declamatory polemical style of the pamphleteers during the American Enlightenment deployed brevity and speed to undermine the distant, alien laws of England, while European intellectuals from Voltaire to Friedrich Schiller used the intimate form of a letter addressed to their fellow citizens to bring their arguments closer to people estranged from monarchs who ruled from afar.

For all of Buddhism's emphasis on peace achieved through the abolition of ego and desire, the Buddha himself was the most contentious founder of any major religion. In one of the many debates the Buddha had with the Brahmins of his day, he explicitly takes on the arbitrary foundation power rests upon, addressing a Brahmin named Assalayana. "But, Assalayana, the brahmins' brahmin-women are plainly seen having their periods, becoming pregnant, giving birth, and nursing [their children]. And yet the brahmins, being born through the birth canal, say, 'Brahmins are the superior caste.' " You might call this *argumentum ab corpore*—an argument from the body. You find it in Montaigne—"Kings and philosophers shit." It is in Shakespeare's deconstruction, in *King Lear,* of Lear's kingship to the humbling biological reality of being a "poor, bare, forked animal." In the 1960s, artists and political activists deployed bodily functions against the entrenched social and political forms of the day. The Living Theater's performance piece *Paradise Now* used nudity as consciousness-raising strategy. Michel Foucault's argument about the human body being a literal, physical atlas of the effects of social and political power is probably the terminus point of this lengthy historical argument that, in fact, shuts down argument.

An argument from the body occurs when a power imbalance makes reasoned argument impossible. Such an argument falls into the larger category of changing the framework of debate entirely. The philosopher of science Thomas Kuhn defined as a "paradigm shift" the moment when a scientific worldview gives way to another worldview with which it has no continuity and which seems to have come from another reality—a shift from Newtonian to Einsteinian physics, for example. Historical change is even more radical. Whenever the status quo is threatened, argument is not simply transformed. It becomes suspended. Here, from Matthew 22:23–33, are the Sadducees trying to draw Jesus into an argument in hopes of refuting his claims of truth:

> That same day the Sadducees, who say there is no resurrection, came to him with a question. "Teacher," they said, "Moses told us that if a man dies without having children, his brother must marry the widow and raise up offspring for him. Now there were seven brothers among us. The first one married and died, and since he had no children, he left his wife to his brother. The same thing happened to the second and third brother, right on down to the seventh. Finally, the woman died. Now then, at the resurrection, whose wife will she be of the seven, since all of them were married to her?"
>
> Jesus replied, "You are in error because you do not know the Scriptures or the power of God. At the resurrection people will neither marry nor be given in marriage; they will be like the angels in heaven. But about the resurrection of the dead—have you not read what God said to you, 'I am the God of Abraham, the God of Isaac, and the God of Jacob'? He is not the God of the dead but of the living."
>
> When the crowds heard this, they were astonished at his teaching.

It is likely that, rather than being astonished at Christ's teaching, the crowds were amazed at his audacity in sweeping away the vision of reality they had accepted and lived by until that moment. No logical, rhetorical, evidentiary response can be made to Christ's claims. They are as discontinuous from the Sadducees' argument as the theory of relativity is from Newton's three laws.

For argument to exist, the parties on each or every side have to share the same reality. Sometimes the shouting that results when they do not is the product of an ontological error. Sometimes it is the dawn of a new way of looking at reality.

I the art of argument

"When, O Catiline, do you mean to stop abusing our patience?"

"Our conscience is absolutely clear."

"Before I start taking questions, I want to open it up with a couple of comments about what we saw and heard yesterday."

The first sentence is from one of Cicero's famous Catilinarian speeches, in which he makes his argument on the Roman Senate floor against Catiline, a senator accused of plotting a coup d'état. The legendary Roman polemicist uses "our" to identify himself with all Romans, to present all Romans as being manipulated, and to make Catiline stand in isolation, outside the community.

In the second sentence, Benito Mussolini, in his "Speech to the People of Rome," delivered after Italy's declaration of war on France and Britain, employs the first-person-plural pronoun to create the illusion that the dictator and the people have fused into a single, mighty will driven by a pure conscience.

The third example is the first sentence of Barack Obama's 2008 speech about race, a speech that weaves, like American democracy itself, from "I" to "we" to "they" and back again, the speaker's first person fluidly changing place with the country's first-person plurality. The first-person-plural pronoun audaciously implies that the speaker is but a vessel of collective truth, a truth validated by his own experience, at once singular and inclusive. Obama seemed to have resigned himself to the fact that feeling, in this case democratic feeling, is the midwife of a convincing argument.

As a rhetorical tactic, "we" seems like a quaint convention of yesteryear. It reached a peak of self-conscious utility in the writing of the literary critic Lionel Trilling, during the heyday of the postwar liberal consensus: "When we say that a movement is 'bankrupt of ideas,' " Trilling wrote, "we are likely to suppose that it is at the end of its powers."

Trilling's "we," however, was not Obama's "we"; it was not the idealistic embodiment of the general public. It was the "we" of a small intellectual caste, highly influential in its own rarefied precincts. That authoritative "we," glowing with the cachet it confers, has always been a highly effective strategy of argument itself. When the *New York Review of Books* ran a six-hundred-plus-word reply to a piece Joan Didion had published there, Didion responded with two: "Oh, wow." Behind her insouciant gesture was Didion's membership in a coterie that had the power to publish, or not publish, the reply to Didion's essay in the first place.

But embedded in Didion's dismissive back of the hand was not only her declaration of belonging to a dominant social group. She was also making it clear that she was a registered practitioner of a dominant intellectual style. "Before you leave the house, look in the mirror and take one thing off," Coco Chanel advised young women. If you've got it, Didion was saying, it is déclassé to flaunt it. Better to leave it out altogether. As we shall see, the power of an argument is often certified by the exclusiveness of a style.

Yet "we" did, and sometimes still does, serve an even more important argumentative purpose. Leaving aside the question of power that the first-person plural raises,[*] "we" performs,

---

[*] A related issue is the absence of agreement about what should be used as a generic pronoun. See my earlier footnote.

among other things, the simple function of establishing a shared reality. "We" meant that fundamental facts did not have to be debated before an argument could begin. The two sides didn't disagree on whether a pandemic existed, for example. At one time people didn't even disagree on what constituted unpublishable expressions of raw emotion.

When the virtual Democratic National Convention in the summer of 2020 used "We the People" as its motto, one thing certain was that at least half the country did not consider itself included in the collective pronoun in that context.

Psychologists use the term "source monitoring" to describe the process by which people distinguish between the sources of a particular memory. Is it based on real events, or derived from a dream? Did it arise from an overheard story or from a movie or a book? One of the effects of trauma is that source monitoring goes haywire. Awash as we are in social media that offer a teeming hodgepodge of information, entertainment, fabrication, prevarication, rumor, and propaganda, it sometimes seems as though society itself has been traumatized by the dissolving boundaries of what is considered real. "We" can hardly exist when "I" is so fluid.

That is the general situation today. It is what argument is up against. But this predicament makes an authentic argument all the more necessary and essential. "Makhloket l'shem shamayim," the rabbis say in the Talmud: "argument for the sake of heaven." It is an argument made for the sole purpose of getting at the truth, without consideration of power, status, moral rightness, or reputation—all factors that can ruin a shared understanding that the facts in question are genuine facts. Though the postwar liberal consensus has gone the way of the typewriter and the telephone, people making an argument still use "we" or "our," for good or ill, not only to invoke a shared reality with their audience but to imply that their argument is a neutral search for the truth. The premise might be easily used for disingenuous purposes, but that only proves its power. Robert Frost said that a poem begins in delight and ends in wisdom. A cogent argument begins in the private delight of an "I" roused to intellectual action, and ends with an urgent appeal to the collective wisdom of "we."

The Exclusiveness of Style

In the turbulent July of 2020, *Harper's* magazine published a short document signed by 143 writers, journalists, and academics called "A Letter on Justice and Open Debate." The purpose of the letter was to protest cancel culture, an atmosphere in which people's careers, and sometimes lives, were ruined when they were exposed and shamed for what you might call spilled inwardness: for having dropped a remark on Twitter, or in a private meeting or conversation, that was construed as socially harmful and then made public. The new prosecutorial style—or style of moral redress, depending on your perspective—had its origins in the #MeToo movement, which caused the professional downfall and personal ruination of a number of prominent men. Here, too, "elite" opinion (the general public did not seem particularly exercised by the new set of circumstances) was divided between those who felt that such men got what they had long deserved in a culture that tolerated the male domination of women and those who believed that the punishment often exceeded the crime.

Hurtful comments randomly made were not the only words that incurred retribution, however. In the fall of 2018, a writer named Ian Buruma, the editor of the *New York Review of Books,* appeared to have been forced to resign for publishing a long, self-exculpatory essay by Jian Ghomeshi, a Canadian media personality who had been acquitted of sexual assault charges two years earlier. Then, in June 2020, James Bennet, the editor of the *New York Times* editorial page, was fired by the liberal newspaper after he published an op-ed by Tom Cotton, Republican senator from Arkansas, arguing for the use of the American military in repressing the violent riots that had followed some of the Black Lives Matter demonstrations.

In retrospect, the febrile arguments set off by both incidents are studies in how personal the true causes of public arguments can be. In response to an interviewer who asked about the allegations made by more than twenty women that Ghomeshi had punched, choked, and bitten them, Buruma remarked that "sexual behavior is a many-faceted business." And Bennet was in an intense, if discreet, competition for the paper's top editorial position, soon to be vacated, as well as the principal figure in a potentially onerous defamation lawsuit being pursued by Sarah Palin against the *Times,* the cause being an unsigned editorial into which Bennet had inserted a statement accusing Palin of inciting the shooting of Congresswoman Gabby Giffords in 2011, a factual error that Bennet had had to publicly apologize for.

Still, the professional demise of both men happened as highly visible instances of exposure, shaming, and revenge were accelerating, and in the eyes of the *Harper's* writers this new phenomenon of instant public reprisal, driven by social media, posed a threat to free expression. They declared that "the free exchange of information and ideas, the lifeblood of a liberal society . . . [is] daily becoming more constricted." Liberal culture, the writers argued, had hardened into intolerance, punishment, and shaming of those with "opposing views."

The letter is just over five hundred words and uses some form of the first-person-plural pronoun eighteen times. The use of the first-person-plural pronoun of course always raises the question of who that "we" represents. In the letter, the identity of "we" is transparent. It is meant to stand for the supposedly elite group of signatories who are presuming to write on behalf of the country's highest ideals. This declaration of "we" immediately establishes a framework of power alongside a specific rhetoric of argument. Thus it raises proprietary questions about the language of formal, public argument.

It bears repeating: Argument is not some high-minded, rarefied form of human interaction. It is shaped by the historical context in which argument is practiced. And the language of a particular moment in time shapes the arguments of that time.

You can find another indication of the *Harper's* signatories' status beyond the collective pronoun in the style of their argument. Steeped in irony and paradox, it has one goal: to prove that its opponents are in truth practicing what they are preaching against.

That polemical tactic is an exceptional moment in the history of rhetoric. Not once in Aristotle's exhaustive survey of the techniques of persuasion does he discuss using opponents' own premises—not their conduct but their intellectual premises, embedded in their very language—against them. Aristotle's omission is curious since the principle of dramatic irony, in which the ancient Greek audience was able to comprehend a character's destiny while the character remained unaware of it, was inscribed in his intellectual genes. Yet the idea that the construction of an argument ironically undermined it, or that an argument led to a conclusion that paradoxically annulled it, never seems to have occurred to him. In our time, however, an argument resting on the principle of irony and paradox has been the style of American intellectuals for about seventy years.

After the Second World War, the American liberal intelligentsia became divided into roughly two sides. On one side were liberals, who shunned communism. On the other were progressives, who often marched under the liberal banner yet who either tolerated communist values or embraced them. The situation was further complicated by the fact that some progressives knew about Stalin's atrocities but remained communists, while others opposed Stalin but stayed sympathetic to communism; the latter group were known to those who opposed communism as fellow travelers.

To round out the complexity, a subset of people existed who referred to themselves as anti-anti-communists. They ran the gamut from principled, anti-Soviet democratic socialists who abhorred right-wing Red-baiting to closet communists who hid behind a seemingly principled stand against right-wing extremism.

Add to these twisting levels of meaning the sense, instilled by the experience of war, that the best-laid plans and most admirable ideals could be blown apart in a second, and you arrive at the dominant style of postwar liberal argumentation: irony and paradox.

Reinhold Niebuhr was the philosopher of such tragic irony. He believed that liberal individualists, for example, embrace a science and technology that are indifferent to the individual and pose a threat to liberalism. Thinking of the use and abuse of American power overseas, he argued that American idealism was often "cruelly refuted by history." As for the fight against communism itself, a nuclear age all but guaranteed that if it continued, the battle for freedom would have the consequence of obliterating earth and its inhabitants.

As Ralph Ellison, the novelist of tragic irony, put it in *Invisible Man:* "Beware of those who speak of the *spiral* of history; they are preparing a boomerang. Keep a steel helmet handy." Mike Tyson phrased it even more plainly: "Everybody has a plan until they get punched in the mouth."

In the eyes of some conservatives of the time, "liberal anticommunism" was a contradiction. For the liberals who defined themselves by the phrase, however, Lionel Trilling most notably, such a seeming paradox came from a complicated habit of mind signifying a thought process that could—as F. Scott

Fitzgerald once defined "the test of a first-rate intelligence"—"hold two opposed ideas in the mind at the same time, and still retain the ability to function."

Though perhaps weakened by time, perhaps even a faint caricature of its former vitality, the style of the *Harper's* letter displays irony and paradox as the proof of its membership in a dominant social group.

Describing their adversaries' commitment to exposing and rooting out injustice, the *Harper's* signatories write, "This needed reckoning has also intensified a new set of moral attitudes and political commitments that tend to weaken our norms of open debate and toleration of differences in favor of ideological conformity. As we applaud the first development, we also raise our voices against the second."

The signatories say they welcome the new social movements, then they expose what they believe to be the irony of the repressive atmosphere that such sentiments of political liberation are causing. And then they embody in a single rhetorical flourish the liberating near-paradox they have just explained: "As we applaud the first development, we also raise our voices against the second." The impression they are attempting to make is clear. Not only are the signatories arguing for intellectual tolerance of opposing views. They are, in their language—they applaud while they protest—practicing them.

They are, they believe, laying bare a paralyzing Niebuhrian tragedy. The protesters' dreams of equality and justice will lead to conditions that will, in Niebuhr's phrase, "cruelly refute" them. "Resistance must not be allowed to harden into its own brand of dogma or coercion." Beware the boomerang of history. After warning that resistance is becoming its own brand of dogma or coercion, the *Harper's* signatories assert that this style on the part of the new "resisters" is precisely one "which right-wing demagogues are already exploiting." You think, they are saying to their opponents, that you are combating your adversaries. In fact you are enabling their tactics by practicing them yourselves.

This prepares us for the conclusion of the letter, in which the writers assert an absolute equivalence between the "repressive government" of a fascist state and the "intolerant society" created, in their eyes, by liberal excesses.

Not long after the *Harper's* letter appeared, a response was published in an online magazine, the *Objective.* The difference between the two arguments is something like the difference between the Sadducees' challenge to Jesus and Jesus's stunningly unconnected response. Just as the Sadducees seek to undermine Jesus's idea of the resurrection by interpreting it in a literal, worldly, almost humorous way—Will we have to keep passing around our one wife among ourselves?—the *Harper's* signatories attempt to instruct their adversaries in the ironic contradictions of their position: Don't you see that you are as repressive as the most repressive politics? The *Objective* writers, however, respond with passionate sincerity.

Whereas the *Harper's* letter abounded with the first-person plural, the *Objective's* response uses one form or another of that pronoun a mere seven times, though the response is three times as long as the original letter. The contrast might have been unintentional, but the implication is striking. The *Objective* represents an evolving plurality of voices that has yet to coalesce into a new status quo. Diversity and tolerance are, perhaps ostentatiously, built into this lack of we-ness, whose ranks continue to grow and to shift. The *Objective,* its signatories are saying, does not need to prove its commitment to free discourse. Its lack of closed doors, along with its fluid heterogeneity, removes the need to do that.

This is what we might call an appeal to the optics of argument, just as the invocation of "we" in the *Harper's* letter attempts to shape readers' perception of what it is saying. Of the *technique* of argument, there is very little in the *Objective's* response. The irony and paradox that are the mark of an official cultural caste are entirely absent. Instead the *Objective's* tone is ardent, earnest, and sincere—rhetorical qualities that have always been associated not with elites but with an insurgent class below the elites.

With its title "A More Specific Letter on Justice and Open Debate," the letter offers a combative counterthrust to the *Harper's* letter. "More specific" implies that the *Harper's* signatories are writing in an older style, one characterized by windy generalizations and ritualistic nods to abstract intellectual pieties.

The *Objective* writers, on the other hand, are going to call particular details by their name. As if replacing a telescope with a magnifying glass, they answer insinuations of irony with exposures of hypocrisy. Describing the *Harper's* letter, they write, "The signatories, many of them white, wealthy, and endowed with massive platforms, argue that they are afraid of being silenced, that so-called cancel culture is out of control, and that they fear for their jobs and free exchange of ideas, even as they speak from one of the most prestigious magazines in the country." Having exchanged the genteel kid gloves of intellectual understatement for the boxing gloves of straightforward accusation, the *Objective*'s letter gradually develops into a specific, real-life catalogue of instances in which, the writers argue, some of the prominent *Harper's* writers did not practice the openness that they are advocating: "In fact, a number of the signatories have made a point of punishing people who have spoken out against them, including . . ."

I hardly want to push the analogy to the Sadducees' confrontation with Christ too far—there is nothing Christlike about the *Objective*'s accusatory tone—but the two instances have fundamental formal similarities, if not essential ones. The Sadducees, an elite stratum of priests, point with an ironic wink to a paradox in the idea of resurrection. Christ answers with ardent sincerity. These are not just rival eschatologies— two competing visions of mortal and eternal life. They are two rhetorical styles that have no point of convergence.

The issue between the *Harper's* and *Objective* writers was one of power—not a question of who gets to talk but of what style gets to be dominant. And when power is the only framework for language, argument becomes impossible. Victory is wrested, not earned and then agreed to. This is an old story: displays of irony are being replaced by cries of hypocrisy. Power itself is being defined as corruption and weakness, while weakness is trying on the accoutrements of power. Insurrections are always roaring with earnest outpourings of feeling, while established thoughts and sentiments, over time, retreat behind moats and ramparts of coded meaning. Of course, people sympathetic to neither side might be tempted to characterize the latter as the complacent harrumphing of the members of a private club and the former as the bellicose resentment of outsiders yearning to be let in. There is always another argument to be made beyond the borders of any particular argument.

The exchange between the *Harper's* and the *Objective's* signatories came to mind after the visceral first presidential debate between Donald Trump and Joe Biden. In that moment you saw a parallel motion to the *Harper's/Objective* argument, a movement *away* from comfortable, staid coded meaning to all-out expressionism. It was argument returning to the foul rag-and-bone shop of its sources in the human ego.

The feelings of fear and rage the debate that night aroused in people of all political stripes laid bare argument's DNA. Since argument is ontological, a biological necessity masquerading as an intellectual obligation or compulsion, you often recall a particular argument in existential rather than intellectual terms. You walk away from an argument never remembering its specific elements, but feeling intensely whether you have been vanquished or vindicated. As Cicero knew, the emotional aftermath of an argument is more vital to its success than its content; the most effective arguments use reason and judgment to displace reason and judgment with feeling. This is why in Shakespeare's *Julius Caesar,* Mark Antony ends his cunning funeral oration over Caesar's body by allowing his audience to sink into the emotional condition his argument has created for them:

O judgment! thou art fled to brutish beasts,
And men have lost their reason. Bear with me;
My heart is in the coffin there with Caesar,
And I must pause till it come back to me. (3.2.114–117)

At the presidential debate that night, both candidates spoke in a language of feeling that left it to the audience to find words to describe it. The formal niceties of an argument mask the emotions and ego-energies animating it, but that night the niceties were stripped away. It was a presidential debate directed by David Lynch: *Blue Velvet* Meets *Red Burlap.* But it could have occurred only at a moment when the dominant rhetorical style that sets the tone for public argument was in flux. For Trump himself had assimilated the energies—or was it the reverse?—of the *Objective*'s insurgent tone.

In watershed moments, argument returns to its ragged, street-fighting roots.

Good but Not Nice

It was John Locke, in his *Essay Concerning Human Understanding,* the seminal document of democratic psychology, who laid out what are now known as the "ad" fallacies in the logic of argument. These are *ad verecundiam, ad ignorantiam,* and *ad hominem.* The first is an argument that looks to experts or to the arguer's own high social status to prove its point. The second is an argument that something is true because it has not been proven false—arguments for and against the existence of God both argue ad ignorantiam. The last everyone knows: it is an attack on an opponent's character.

Against these fallacious modes of disputation, Locke placed his ideal of argument: *argumentum ad judicium.* This he defined as argument that was supported by "the foundations of knowledge and probability," an argument based on facts and logic, in other words. It was a neutral and amiable search for the truth, something like the Hindu notion of Vada, or the Talmudic idea of "argument for the sake of heaven." Locke's ideal argument was one that was unaffected by any context or factor outside the intellectual rules of argument themselves. That was his conception of democracy, too. He saw it as a political system that built consensus on the solid foundation of shared facts and a general agreement about the possibilities the facts could or could not support, or could or could not lead to.

For human beings, however, fallible creatures that we are, the so-called "fallacies" of argumentation operate more like essential tips on how to mount an effective argument. If we were all rational, logical beings, guided by the greatest good for the greatest number of people, then we would easily be convinced by rational, logical argument based on knowledge and reasoning. But as Aristotle knew, we are amalgams of feelings, impulses, and intuitions.

So much energy is spent these days pining for the "lost art of argument," as though this Apollonian ideal of debate had been replaced by the three "ads," the most frequent falling-off being the ad hominem argument. People who implore us plangently to put argument back on top again, sometimes claim a distinction between argument and persuasion. Argument in this formulation is good; persuasion is bad. Argument presents a person's case for something based on Locke's ideal of evidence and logic. Persuasion, on the other hand, relies on dishonest advertising, crooked political rhetoric, outright propaganda. Sometimes the distinction is reversed. Argument is associated with a strident, solipsistic propounding of a thesis that amounts to an obsession, while persuasion gently appeals to the rational mind.

But argument has always been suffused with emotional appeals, illogical leaps, personal attacks, misrepresentations of an opponent's position—recall the "bad" Aristotle.

Cicero, who advised that "when you have no basis for argument, abuse the plaintiff," wrote in *De oratore,* "For purposes of persuasion the art of speaking relies wholly upon three things: the proof of our allegations, the winning of our hearer's favour, and the rousing of their feelings to whatever impulse our case may require."

The "proof of our allegations" conforms to Locke's standard of evidence and logic, while the "winning of our hearer's favour" encompasses the tactical use of "we" and the power of style. The "rousing of their feelings to whatever impulse our case may require" is the dark part. It permits the use of the three ads along with whatever else might appeal to the emotions of the audience.

Cicero is at pains to point out that the most effective way of manipulating the audience is to make people aware of at least one of the manipulative techniques, the better to conceal the other two. That way you can coax listeners into relaxing their vigilance: "And because . . . there are three methods of bringing people to hold our opinion, instruction or persuasion or appeal to their emotions, one of these three methods we must openly display . . . whereas the two remaining methods should be interfused throughout the whole of the structure of our speeches like the blood in our bodies."

To return to Mark Antony's funeral oration in *Julius Caesar*, that speech is an example of an argument that plays on the emotions of its audience while seeming to respect the preconceived notions of its audience. By repeating "Brutus is an honorable man" again and again, each time after gently insinuating the opposite, Antony performs the remarkable feat of using the audience's own outrage to refute its own bias. But only one of "the three methods of bringing people to hold our opinion" is apparent, in this case, "the winning of our hearer's favour"—the power of Mark Antony's style.

Closer to home, I myself have tried to manipulate you, dear reader, while seeming to make an impartial argument.

In the paragraph above, where I describe the desire to recapture what I call "the lost art of argument," I tried to give the impression that I was presenting that case neutrally, but I deliberately chose language that was anything but neutral. I wrote that such people were "pining" for the lost art of argument, whereas if I were one of those people I would describe us as "hoping" for its restoration. "Pining" connotes a mind destabilized by forlorn wanting, while "hoping" is a positive state to be in. I referred to such a conception of argument as "Apollonian" thereby dismissing it as fantastical. I said these people "implore us plangently . . . to put argument back on top again"—"plangently" and "implore" indicating the same distressed mental state as "pining," and putting "argument back on top again" resonating, I hope, with coarse ambition.

No effective argument has ever been a model of either logical and evidentiary probity or politeness. If the best arguments were people, they would have the temperaments of prophets. They would be good, but not nice.

Lamenting, like the writers of the *Harper's* letter, what they called a rising counterculture driven by "a fundamental belief in power" that "chills open debate," the editors of the *Economist* recently argued for a return to the time when American "leaders like Frederick Douglass and Martin Luther King" relied on "vigorous protest and relentless argument," a time when liberalism prevailed because its adherents believed in "progress through argument and debate."

But in fact—suspect any argument that uses "in fact," as if the point the arguer is trying to prove were a settled feature of reality—Douglass's arguments often depended on his heart-rending account of the suffering wreaked on the bodies of slaves by Edward Covey, a "Negro-breaker," and on Douglass's description of his life-changing defiance of Covey.

As for King, you could count the times he actually debated someone on the fingers of both hands. His speeches were appeals to the heart and to the ear. The most cogent part of his "argument" was the great numbers of black people he summoned to marches and protests. Its premise was that either black people were empowered or, as James Baldwin put it, "The Negroes of this country may never be able to rise to power, but they are very well placed indeed to precipitate chaos and ring down the curtain on the American dream." In other words, the premise of King's argument was that if his argument prevailed there would be no role for argument to play at all.

Both Douglass and King knew that effective argument extended far beyond (I had to pause over the polemical value of "far"—does it intensify my point nicely, or does it betray an insecure position by its emphatic quality?) the boundaries of shared knowledge and accepted logic.

Fifteen years after Lincoln issued the Emancipation Proclamation, Douglass said in a public speech that Lincoln "was preeminently the white man's president, entirely devoted to the welfare of white men." Hopeful of success in the South, King despaired of it in the North, observing even after the passage of the Civil Rights Act and the Voting Rights Act one year later that white liberal leaders in the North "welcomed me to their cities, and showered praise on the heroism of Southern Negroes. Yet . . . only the language was polite; the rejection was firm and unequivocal."

Neither man shared the *Economist* editors' rosy faith in the power of argument. The goal of their arguments, such as they were, was to bring society to an impasse, like that between the Sadducees and Jesus, after which conflict could finish what argument had started. Having gathered up emotion where

they could, they clearly decided that social and political arguments need to be resolved by some degree of organized emotion.

Now the *Economist* editors might respond that the point I
have made exists comfortably alongside the point that they
were making. They never said that argument was a rational
process that led, rationally, to social change—that was my own
straw man. They merely said that in the large scheme of things,
argument often had the effect of leading to social change. And
they would be right. Up to a point.

But What About You?

The most notorious of the ads is the ad hominem argument.
In American society, where individuality is the highest good,
and therefore an intimate attack on an individual becomes a
feared and lethal bad, arguing ad hominem gets more roundly
condemned even as it becomes more widely used.

Ad hominem argument can be divided into three catego-
ries. One is Twitter's favorite: the claim that someone's position on something cannot be valid, not because that person's
actions contradict his prescriptions but because he is too rot-
ten to be credible. The second is that a particular position
merely reflects the proponent's self-interest. And the third is

known as *tu quoque,* "you also," or as we say, "What about you?" If you tell your children to get off their computer and phone screens, lecture them on the dire cognitive effects of too much screen time, and then go back to your smartphone, you lay yourself open to the tu quoque charge.

The standard definition of tu quoque is that it is a charge of hypocrisy. When you make a tu quoque argument you are accusing your opponent of behavior that undermines the principles animating his own argument. The authors of the *Objective*'s letter, for example, accused one of the signatories of the *Harper's* letter of working to deny academic tenure to someone who held different beliefs from hers even as she was decrying a cancel culture that punished people for holding different beliefs from the majority. In our moment of highly personalized culture, where fractured egos seem to have replaced fracturing ideologies, tu quoque has become a dominant argumentative style.

The dubious advantage of being the target of a tu quoque argument is that a refutation of it can dispense with the labor of constructing a counterargument. All that is required is for the person being attacked to prove that he was either not being a hypocrite or not doing what he has been accused of doing.

But the target could also offer an intellectual response to a tu quoque argument instead of a personal one. The respondent could practice the famous dictum, reputed to have been formulated by Thomas Aquinas, "When you meet a contradiction, make a distinction." In our ultra-personal era, learning how to turn contradictions into distinctions is the rhetorical equivalent of CPR.

In response to Susan Sontag's *Against Interpretation,* for example, a critic might have argued that her own argument for the independence of a work of art from moral meaning was itself a moral statement—rather than helping us understand the world, Sontag argued, art helps us live in the world—thus she contradicts herself.

But Sontag's response to such a hypothetical challenge to her argument is right there in her essay, where she introduces a new level of meaning beyond morality—where she makes a distinction rather than committing a contradiction.

Elia Kazan, she writes, the director of the original Broadway production of Tennessee Williams's *A Streetcar Named Desire,* surrendered to the expectation that a work of art convey a clear moral meaning when he wrote in his notes on the play that Stanley Kowalski represented "the sensual and vengeful barbarism that was engulfing our culture, while Blanche DuBois stood for [endangered and refined] Western civilization." Sontag, by contrast, understood the play as being about "a handsome brute named Stanley Kowalski and a faded mangy belle named Blanche DuBois," the way an abstract expressionist painter would understand his painting not as, say, a heroic existential gesture but as an accumulation of brushstrokes. Sontag's account of *Streetcar* might be a moral statement in its resistance to the imposition of moral meaning, but that would be a moral statement in an entirely different category from the one it is arguing against. It would be a moral statement entirely divorced from any type of practical morality.

A more effective tu quoque argument against Sontag might cite the place in her essay where she declares that the act of interpreting a work of art is "the revenge of the intellect upon the world." Having the benefit of nearly sixty years' hindsight, including a full-length biography of Sontag, a critic might argue that Sontag's lifework was itself the revenge she took with her intellect on the world. Such a reductively ad hominem retort might suit the intensely personal world we inhabit now. But it would reach too far beyond the particularity of Sontag's work to be very convincing as a rebuttal to it.

Like our hypothetical critic of Sontag, the authors of the *Harper's* letter tried to use their targets' premises to undermine their argument. They described a contradiction between what they saw as their opponents' commitment to diversity and their opponents' efforts to stifle free speech on the way to attaining their goal. But in their response, the *Objective*'s signatories refused to make a distinction where the *Harper's* letter saw a contradiction. Instead they hurled back a classic tu quoque, accusing the *Harper's* writers of practicing what they were preaching against. What was at stake between the two sides was not a moral or an intellectual proposition, but something beyond moral or intellectual dispute. Each side insisted that what the other side said was made invalid by what the other side did.

We are in the realm of Pericles' Funeral Oration, where actions must prove the validity of words even before words are spoken. Each side seems unconsciously to be making an argument within the argument it thinks it is having. Both sides are claiming, "Time will tell."

"We" and "You" and the River of Time

The *Harper's* signatories believed that the status quo accommodated, even promoted change and diversity through open debate. The *Objective* writers believed that the status quo only tolerated debate that maintained the status quo.

Forgive one more formulation, but you might call this an argument to the past versus an argument to the future: *argumentum ad tempore*—an argument to time. From Eve carefully contesting with God in the primal garden, to Aeschylus's

itician will ever mention death, unless it is in connec-
th an opponent, but democratic politics in the twenty-
ntury is based on how people regard time, and thus on
ey approach the fact of mortality. This is why political
nt, like every argument, has to make its appeal on the
emotional level.

hen Vincent Benet's nearly forgotten "The Devil and
Webster"—once a staple of the high school curriculum—
nly work of American literature that turns on an argu-
hat is also *about* the art of argument, and particularly
n argument to time.

n the 1840s, the story has a simple plot. A New England
named Jabez Stone who has fallen on hard times sells
to the devil in exchange for several years of prosperity.
ose years are up, the devil comes to collect, and Stone,
ng the deal he has made, hires the celebrated real-life
and orator Daniel Webster to get him off the hook.

ster begins by arguing for, in effect, lack of jurisdiction,
g that because the devil is not a citizen of the United
Stone cannot "be forced into the service of a foreign
The devil's response is a model of a defense based on
nd evidence and homespun irony. He is indeed an

Athena arguing with the conservative Furies in the *Eumenides,*
to Cicero taking on a corrupt Roman aristocracy, to Shakespeare's Coriolanus the patrician deploring the democratic
wave of the future, to Martin Luther's ninety-nine theses refuting the Catholic Church—the underlying shape of argument
is often between two ways of looking at time.

You might even say that if argument had a platonic form, or
an archetype, it would follow along such temporal lines. To
the extent that people still argue about literary fiction, for example, traditionalists favor realism, which assumes that tran-
sient social details embody immutable human essences. That is
an argument that identifies a changelessness at the heart of
time which consoles us for living lives that always, no matter
when we die, end in the middle. Advocates of experimental
fiction, by contrast, make an argument for surrendering ourselves to changes in the way the cultural vanguard perceives
reality.

The intense and critical social arguments raging around the
pandemic as I write this are arguments to time. They ultimately present one fundamental choice: accept death as part of life
and find a way to keep living, or do everything you can to
forestall death, an effort that is also part of life. In the former
case, you are born with essential meaning and spend your life
striving to uncover it—the past embodies the future. In the

latter, you change as your circumstances change—the future takes primacy over the past.

In cultural and intellectual life, debate often comes down to a dispute over time. "We stand in need of the moral realism," wrote Lionel Trilling, "which is the product of the free play of the moral imagination." *The* moral realism; *the* free play of *the* moral imagination. The definite articles argue that these three qualities have always existed; they are a permanent feature of the human intellect, and they are what "serious"—Trilling's talismanic word—art must possess.

To those certitudes, Sontag replied in *Against Interpretation:* "What is important now is to recover our senses. We must learn to *see* more, to *hear* more, to *feel* more" (emphasis in the original). Sontag's "now" defies Trilling's definite articles. The italicized verbs signifying the operation of the senses carry Sontag's words into experience, into the present and away from abstractions like "the moral imagination." In the same way, the *Harper's* writers want to hang on to a moment in time, while the *Objective* writers want to move beyond it. The implications of irony are static; the exposures of hypocrisy are dynamic.

Conservative and liberal positions are, in the end, two different ways of looking at time. The agrarian/industrial schism

at the heart of American politics, whi[ch] red versus blue conflict of today, is e[ ] between staying close to time-honor[ed] the rhythms of nature and using scie[nce] propel humanity into a particular con[ ]

The campaign slogans in recent ele[ctions] just to the country's fundamental div[ ] argument about past, present, and fut[ure]

Bill Clinton's slogan was "For Peopl[e] H. W. Bush's was "A Proud Traditio[n] New Millennium" went Al Gore's, w[ ] sponded with "Compassionate Cons[ervatism] campaign used "Change We Can Beli[eve in] Cain's "Country First," while his se[ ] Mitt Romney's "Restore Our Futur[e] had "Make America Great Again" ([ ] Reagan) while Hillary Clinton used "[ ]

Voters did not gravitate to one sid[e] the basis of a point of policy. These t[ ] ciety reflect two different attitudes [ ] time in human life—you abide by w[ ] brace change as it happens. This is [ ] conservatives appeal to older voters a[nd]

Enter[ ]

No p[ ] tion [ ] first c[ ] how t[ ] argum[ ] deepe[ ]

Ste[ ] Danie[ ] is the [ ] ment [ ] about [ ]

Set [ ] farme[r] his so[ ] After t[ ] regret[ ] lawyer[ ]

We[ ] claimi[ng] States[ ] prince[ ] logic [ ]

American, he argues. "When the first wrong was done to the first Indian, I was there. When the first slaver put out for the Congo, I stood on her deck. . . . 'Tis true the North claims me for a Southerner, and the South for a Northerner, but I am neither. I am merely an honest American like yourself—and of the best descent—for, to tell the truth, Mr. Webster, though I don't like to boast of it, my name is older in this country than yours."

On this particular point, the devil's argument carries the day. The case goes to trial, with Webster eventually prevailing by arguing that American freedom encompasses both good and bad behavior, and that its splendor lies in the freedom to work for positive change.

Webster's slowly soaring rhetoric makes its deepest appeal to elemental feelings: "And [Webster] began with the simple things that everybody's known and felt—the freshness of a fine morning when you're young, and the taste of food when you're hungry, and the new day that's every day when you're a child. He took them up and he turned them in his hands. They were good things for any man. But without freedom, they sickened."

The country lawyer is returning the bounty of a future to everyone on the jury by describing a shared past. He is making an argument to time. Webster ends his summation with this striking passage. As Benet describes it, Webster "was telling the story and the failures and the endless journey of mankind. They got tricked and trapped and bamboozled, but it was a great journey. And no demon that was ever foaled could know the inwardness of it—it took a man to do that." It took a man, another human being, to "know the inwardness" of human experience. That is to say, it is not enough to appeal to your audience. You have to inhabit them, and you have to give them the illusion of inhabiting you, too. One powerful way to accomplish that is by invoking a universal past, tenderly shared, in order to establish a common mortality.

Let's take a leap into the more recent past and into what has become another work of American folklore. The movie *Saving Private Ryan* might seem no more than a superb story of war, but it ends as a high-stakes argument to time.

In the film's final moments, Captain Miller (played by Tom Hanks) is talking with Private Ryan (Matt Damon) as the two of them face a ferocious battle in which they might be killed. The older man and the young man reminisce about home. Miller says, "Well, when I think of home, I . . . I think of something specific. I think of my, my hammock in the back-yard or my wife pruning the rosebushes in a pair of my old work gloves."

No life full of such treasured memories, he seems to be arguing, could be cracked open like a jug of wine and have all its inwardness spill out, as if love and the memory of love meant nothing. When Private Ryan asks him to "tell me about your wife and those rosebushes," Miller refuses. "No, that one I save just for me."

The two men are having an argument on the most intimate level. Ryan spills out his inwardness to Miller, telling him a ribald story about how he and his three brothers once played a prank on a girl. But there is an undercurrent of violence to the prank, which involves making a travesty of sexual intercourse, the act of conception. It is as if in the heedless vitality of his youth, Ryan is denying the fact of mortality itself. And the prank took place in Ryan's youth, and implies, at the moment when Miller feels that he has used up all his past, that Ryan will have a future, especially since it seems that Miller has, in effect, taken on the responsibility of preserving Ryan's life at the expense of his own.

Most ominous of all, the three brothers who also took part in the prank are now dead. It is all too much for Miller. "No, that one I save just for me." By which he may well mean, "My life is just as worth *saving*, Private Ryan, as yours."

Yet death creeps into Miller's sacred memories anyway. He transforms his fear of lying dead on the battlefield into a memory of lying in a hammock; his cherished recollection of his wife pruning the rosebushes is a symbolic dread of death cutting away his fragile life. "We make out of the quarrel with others, rhetoric," William Butler Yeats wrote, "but of the quarrel with ourselves, poetry." Miller is arguing with himself, with Private Ryan, and with a world that is closing in on him.

Empathy with a Punch

As we have seen, Aristotle spends a good deal of time in the *Rhetoric* explaining how an orator—argument was spoken then, not written—might be able either to produce emotions like anger, fear, and enmity in his audience or to recognize them in the audience and play on them. Though Aristotle deplored the crass theatrics deployed by the orators of his day, he spends most of the *Rhetoric* dispensing advice on how to manipulate the emotions in the same way those orators did. The difference for Aristotle was that he regarded such manipulation as rooted in a science of the emotions, not as a theatrical gambit.

Aristotle thought arguers could arrive at this goal by analyzing how their audience thinks and feels and then shaping their argument to conform to their conception of an audience's inner state. For example, if I am writing an opinion piece arguing against a sudden enthusiasm for medical rationing among liberals, I will have to analyze the mind of a liberal. For the sake of argument, let us assume that delicate conscience will be uppermost, followed by the guilty suspicion that we are all implicated in our aversions, followed by a redoubled assertion of conscience.

Now I have my main line of argument. I will argue that in advocating for medical rationing, liberals are pushing rationalism to an inhuman extreme and betraying their deepest principles—a touch of irony and paradox here—because they are not considering the strong possibility that factors like race, class, and disability may play a role, unconsciously or not, in the decision to allow a patient to die.

Putting yourself in your opponent's shoes in this way has long been a convention of debating. Edmund Burke was widely celebrated for his almost uncanny ability to see every facet of an argument, a gift that was sharpened by both his lifelong passion for the theater and the British convention of requiring the participants of a debate to train for it by switching sides—that is, playing roles. He was so effective at it that *A Vindication of Natural Society,* his satirical argument exposing the limitations of rationalism—composed by Burke in the style of his intellectual target, Lord Bolingbroke—was believed to have been written by Bolingbroke himself. Burke, however, was Burke. In other hands such role-playing often comes down to a mechanical, academic exercise in mental agility.

There is a more imaginative, intuitive way of arguing, and it has to do with the actor's principal tool.

Another Burke, Kenneth, is not well known today. His obscurity is a pity because Burke's *Rhetoric of Motives* and, to a lesser extent, his *Grammar of Motives* are on par with Aristotle's reflections on argument.

Like Aristotle, Burke identified rhetoric with persuasion. As Aristotle did, he found the sources of the art of persuasion everywhere in the human condition, from "courtship" to the quest for social status to politics and beyond. Burke, though, despite his social scientific language, was thinking not only about the theatrics of emotional appeals. He was thinking about argument as a performance in the theater of social life.

Writing directly after the devastation of the Second World War, Burke believed that the timeless human urge to persuade other humans lies in the divisive nature of human society. He saw life as ceaseless conflict and therefore ceaseless argument. He used a Latin phrase to capture the purpose of his life's work on rhetoric: *ad bellum purificandum,* which can mean "toward the purification [eradication] of war" but also "toward the purification [making pure] of the beautiful thing." In his mind, persuasion was a species of war that "purified" military war of its violence and irrationality, and it was a refined art that sought the "beautiful thing" of cooperation through agreement.

In response to division and strife, people have devised myriad forms of cooperation. Some of these fail miserably: in a striking phrase, Burke defines war as "a disease of cooperation." People never stop trying for harmony, though. At the root of every argument is an appeal for human beings to join together around its point, even if they do so in opposition to other human beings. "If men were not apart from one another," Burke writes, "there would be no need for the rhetorician to proclaim their unity." There would be no need, that is, for anyone to try to argue anyone else into agreement with him.

Burke's answer to universal conflict is what he calls "identification." He considers it to be at the heart of effective argument. "Identification ranges from the politician who, addressing an audience of farmers, says, 'I was a farm boy myself,' through the mysteries of social status, to the mystic's identification with the source of all being." Burke's identification is something more than seeing things through an opponent's or an audience's eyes. It is wearing that person's clothes, working at that person's job, sitting in that person's living room. To achieve this entrance into another person's life, Burke took another turn.

Burke never mentions empathy as a quality of identification; he barely mentions the term at all. Like Aristotle, he is too interested in conferring on his theories the demonstrable certainties of science, and the operation, even the existence, of empathy is impossible to quantify. But he comes close to empathy as the central principle of argument in his notion of "dramatism."

To illustrate the centrality of human motivation, Burke turns to the model of a stage play: "We shall use five terms as generating principle of our investigation. They are: Act, Scene, Agent, Agency, Purpose. . . . [A]ny complete statement about motives will offer *some kind of* answers to these five questions: what was done (act), when or where it was done (scene), who did it (agent), how he did it (agency), and why (purpose)."

Burke then goes on to develop a theory of human motivation that he joins to his notion of identification. It has a familiar ring: "all the world's a stage and all the men and women merely players" combined with "put yourself in the other guy's shoes." But what Burke does with his framework is not routine at all. By rooting the practice of argument in the quest for motivation, then putting the quest for motivation in a theatrical framework, he is shifting effective argument away from its roots in rhetoric.

At the time Burke was writing, Method acting was becoming the dominant style of acting on stage and screen. There are many versions of "the Method," but they all share a basic principle. Actors are required to know precisely what motivates their character and what motivates the other characters in every scene. Once the actors find, deep in themselves, some identical form of wanting, the character comes to life.

The ancient Greeks had no term for empathy, despite the fact that "empathy" is derived from an ancient Greek word (it means "passion" or "feeling"). In his exhaustive exploration of the emotions, Aristotle never considered the phenomenon of one person feeling what another was feeling. Such identification with another human being would have been a useless emotion in the ancient world, where life was short, armed conflict incessant, and torture, execution, and enslavement the consequences of military defeat. On the other hand, perhaps empathy came so naturally to ancient people that no one made a fuss about it.

In our modern, capitalist time, so haunted by excesses of ego that blot out other people's inwardness altogether, the nature and function of empathy is a persistent preoccupation.

The psychoanalyst Heinz Kohut had a name for what Burke himself most likely did not recognize he was reaching for. Kohut called it "vicarious introspection." Without that imaginative process, Kohut said, society would fall apart. Kohut considered vicarious introspection an essential therapeutic tool. He liked to illustrate this imaginative leap with the example of encountering a person who was exceptionally tall: "Only when we think ourselves into his place . . . by vicarious introspection, begin to feel his unusual size as if it were our own and thus revive [our own] inner experiences in which we had been unusual or conspicuous, only then do we begun to appreciate the meaning that the unusual size may have for this person and only then have we observed a psychological fact."

This is not the standard role-playing exercise in debate preparation. Imagining yourself into another person's "inwardness" goes beyond thinking. A psychoanalyst named Theodore Jacobs later recast Kohut's example into a hypothetical anecdote in order to make this point:

> A colleague of some renown who . . . was extremely small in stature received a call [for] a consultation. . . . [At] the arranged time the new patient arrived. . . . About to enter the waiting room to greet him, the analyst suddenly stopped at the threshold and, momentarily, stood transfixed. There in front of him was a Paul Bunyan of a figure, fully six feet, eight inches in height, weighing perhaps 260 pounds, and wearing cowboy boots and a ten gallon hat. For several more seconds the analyst looked at

him in silence. Then, with a shrug of his shoulders and a resigned gesture, he motioned toward his office. "Come on in, anyway," he said.

The situation seemed rationally impossible; the analyst thought he could never overcome his feeling of being in the presence of physical strangeness. Then his imagination took a leap into the heart of his own life, into his own sensory memories, in order to understand the person standing before him. "Come on in, anyway."

There is a moment in the construction of an argument when the inwardness of your opponent comes in upon you in a flash. "Come on in, anyway"—let me be you in all the strangeness that I find in you. Once I experience in myself what you must be, then I know how to persuade you.

Let us return to the liberals and their argument for what is essentially euthanasia. I try to identify with them in the deepest sense; I try to vicariously inhabit them as people, not as social or intellectual types. Their stated purpose in advocating for medical rationing is to save lives. Many of them are doctors, and they prize life above all else. This ardent conviction is what has brought them to their position.

I prize life above all else, too. That is my motive for making my argument against them. I think of my deepest fears, and I imagine myself in the situation of my worst fear coming true.

It is everyone's worst fear; this horror lies at the unifying heart of all the diverse, disproportionate, conflicting circumstances in life: the horror of dying.

I describe the situation, during the pandemic, of an elderly woman, an immigrant, impoverished, alone, unable to speak more than rudimentary English. She walks unsteadily into a crowded emergency room in her neighborhood. In her late seventies, obese, coughing and sneezing uncontrollably, she suddenly experiences a heart attack as she sits in the waiting area and needs to be revived.

At the same time, a young white woman is rushed in on a gurney, also unable to breathe but not coughing or sneezing. Her heart rate is low and she has a fever that is rising. The elderly immigrant woman is alone. The white woman has come in with her boyfriend, who is obviously well-heeled and is demanding that she be attended to. Rather than take the chance of himself or any nurses becoming infected with coronavirus, the doctor on call, a white man in his late fifties, exhausted, at the end of a sixteen-hour shift, decides to concentrate all his efforts on trying save the life of the young white woman. He does this instinctively, and the next day, when he recalls the situation and begins to cry, he cannot even explain to himself what his rationalization was for acting the way he did. Was it the critical mass of newspaper pieces and cable news segments justifying medical rationing? Had they joined with his exhaustion and disabled his conscience? The immigrant patient had died, alone, no one able to understand her final words, which she had spoken in her native language. The young white woman, who, it turned out, had had an anaphylactic reaction to something she had eaten, was able to leave the hospital a few hours later.

Now a surefire way to commandeer an argument is to take it in a completely different direction by standing on its head the conventional understanding of the matter at hand. Ever since Plato dismissed the practice of argument as, in effect, false consciousness, and especially today, argument has been defined with distaste as synonymous with noisy bickering. At best—in Aristotle's *Rhetoric,* for example—argument is treated as cold, calculating manipulation. Noisy bickering on one side, cold, calculating hydraulics on the other—if argument matters at all, it seems, that is only because life does not seem able to proceed without it.

I wanted to turn that negative conception of argument upside down, so I redefined argument as everything its detractors claim it is not. Where they see selfishness, I postulate an empathetic surrender to another person. Where they describe conflict and chaos, I paint a picture of resolution and harmony. The idea of "empathy with a punch," by definition a contradiction in terms, challenges conventional notions of language and experience.

But my use of empathy is a sort of pandering in the end, and unconvincing. For one thing, the idea of empathy has become wearyingly banal. In American society, so driven by consumerism and greed, the invocation of empathy has become a ritualistic and mechanical display of moral credentials.

Yet empathy does not necessarily have anything to do with the sensitivity and gentleness popularly attributed to it. Empathy is not the same thing as sympathy. Some of the most empathetic people you will ever meet are business people and lawyers, the latter making use of empathy with a vengeance. Both social types can grasp another person's feelings in an instant, act on them, and clinch a deal or win a trial. The result may well leave the person on the other side feeling anguished or defeated.

And empathy can be an essential quality of sadism. Discerning the most refined degrees of discomfort and pain in another person is the fulcrum of the sadist's pleasure. There is no more empathetic character in literature than Iago, who is able to detect the slightest fluctuation in Othello's emotional state.

As for my heartbreaking example of the elderly immigrant woman dying alone in the hospital, I have cynically and coldly— thank you, Aristotle—made use of two supposedly vulnerable groups, immigrants and women, and of one social group that is widely and loudly disapproved of, the affluent straight white male. I am not so much illustrating empathy as performing a theatrical sympathy and revulsion along approved social lines.

To top it all off, I began by making a gesture of magnanimity toward my opponents, those who advocate medical rationing. I wrote that "their stated purpose in advocating for medical rationing is to save lives. Many of them are doctors, and they prize life above all else." But this is only part of what I believe. I also think that half of them are eugenicists who are pursuing a long-cherished agenda, and half are views-conscious media figures eager to paint as alarming a situation as possible. Still, the gesture of magnanimity, combined with my display of concern for society's most vulnerable people, not only helps strengthen my case for the centrality of empathy in argument, it also makes me seem like a prince of empathy myself. But the fact that I am going to such lengths to make a case for empathy in argument means that I will ruthlessly pursue any means to win my own argument.

And if you believe that I believe *that* argument against myself, I have a homemade herbal supplement I'm eager to sell you. All I really wanted to do just now was to demonstrate empathy with a punch by, as it were, trying to inhabit you as you were reading and arguing with me. And if I constructed an argument against mine only to distract you from a more convincing counterargument, then so much the better.

The definition of "care" in *Webster's Third New International Dictionary* has to be one of the most eloquent and complicated definitions in that vast compendium of the English language. *Webster's* gives the word six shades of meaning:

> 1: a suffering of mind . . . 2a: a burdened or disquieted state of blended preoccupation, uncertainty, apprehension or fear . . . 3: serious attention; esp: attention accompanied by caution, pain, wariness, personal interest, or responsibility . . . 4: regard coming from desire or esteem . . . 5: . . . responsibility for or attention to safety and well-being . . . 6: a person or thing that is an object of attention, anxiety, or solicitude.

These subtle inflections of meaning also reflect the stages of an argument, from conception to completion. Some falsehood, or injury, or violation of decency causes deep unease. A facet of life requires an intensity of attention few people give it, or demands an integrity of attention few people are willing or able to give it. Something in the world arouses a desire to defend it, protect it, restore it, sustain it; this thing under siege is dear; it touches you. You feel responsible for it.

Caring comes in many forms. Few people would hold up Jonathan Swift's lacerating satirical argument "A Modest Proposal" as an example of caring. But the celebrated essay begins with suffering, disquiet, fear; it continues with attention accompanied by pain and a sense of personal responsibility, attention trained on the desire to rescue an esteemed object of compassion.

In the eighteenth century, rationalism's elevation of any policy that led—to use a nineteenth-century formulation—to the greatest pleasure and happiness for the largest number of people degenerated into the practice of often using injurious means to attain lofty ends. Rationalism's sincerest advocates believed that they were fostering good. This made them blind, or numb, to the often perverted consequences of their first principles.

And this was what made so effective Swift's satirical argument that it was sound economic and social policy for impoverished Irish families to sell their children to the wealthy as a table delicacy. As Edmund Burke later would in his *Vindication,* another attack on the presumptions of rationalism, Swift inhabited, empathetically, both his opponents' first principles and his opponents' moral fervor in pursuing them. He shocked them out of their complacency by being more them, morally and intellectually, than they ever imagined they were.

Argument is an ultimate form of caring. That is almost comically counterintuitive, I know. How can an argument be a form of caring when the object of an argument is to demolish the opponent's position, in the course of which any sort of appeal—to authority, to the audience's gullibility, to the character of an opponent—is justified so long as it does not violate the right proportions of logic, evidence, and taste that an argument is built on? How can Swift be biting and caring? I would like to argue that he is.

The philosopher Martin Buber made a spiritual and philosophical distinction between regarding another person as an "It" and seeing that person as a "Thou," or "You." An "It" person is a purely quantifiable and quantified being. The "It" person is demographically, biologically, scientifically fixed in time and space. He or she can be summed up with facts and figures. Think of the difference between your existence in a census and your existence as a person suffused with, as Stephen Vincent Benet put it, "inwardness."

The "Thou" person, however, is a particularity without end. This person exists as a unique human being, irreducible to any statistical category or to any cognitive or behavioral formula. A "Thou" person is impossible to quantify, to sum up.

The best arguments occupy both dimensions. They are Janus-faced entities. In one dimension, they treat their opponent's position solely as an "It." They focus on the facts of the case, the language used to make the argument, the relation of the opponent's argument to its own internal logic, and even to the opponent's publicly verifiable behavior outside the boundaries of the argument.

In the other dimension, the opposing positions share a general moral passion about a particular aspect of reality. The advocates of medical rationing want to save lives. You oppose medical rationing because you too want to save lives. You both begin with an identical passion about, or perhaps outrage over, a particular phenomenon. You both start out with an intuition about what is good and true in that specific situation. You both begin in the mystery of mortality and end in the politics of a specific argument about a specific mortal situation.

This shared moral passion is the opening to the empathetic bond you must form with your opponent before beginning an argument. Certainly such a bond can stop with the apprehension of the other side as an "It," a quantifiable state of mind by which you navigate as you construct an argument that manipulates the audience. But at its best, and at its heart, your argument grasps the state of mind you are seeking to refute as a "Thou," just as you are a "Thou." That visceral, intuitive apprehension of the other side enables you to make your argument a thorough form of understanding theirs—all the better to take it apart.

The imaginative heat of the most powerful arguments does not so much refute or debunk the other side as melt the two sides together. The aim of Shylock's argument for understanding in *The Merchant of Venice* is to fuse himself and his antagonists into a common experience of humanity: "Hath not a Jew eyes? Hath not a Jew hands, organs, dimensions, senses, affections, passions? Fed with the same food, hurt with the same weapons, subject to the same diseases, healed by the same means, warmed and cooled by the same winter and summer as a Christian is?" We *all* believe that we harbor the angels of our better nature. (Abraham Lincoln.) At long last, we *all* are outraged by the spectacle of the absence of a sense of decency. (Joseph N. Welch cross-examining Senator Joseph McCarthy.) We *all* have a dream of peace and harmony. (Martin Luther King.) Not every potent argument has to possess such a high degree of vicarious introspection. But every potent argument aspires to it. And the more fundamental your grasp of who your opponent is, the more embracing the "we"; the more embracing the we, the less consequential the question of dominant rhetorical style.

Swift concluded his satire by declaring that he wrote it "having no other motive than the public good of my country, by advancing our trade, providing for infants, relieving the poor, and giving some pleasure to the rich." How startled Ireland's English aristocratic overlords must have been to read such a precise description of how they understood their own motives, following such a savage exposure of the consequences of their motives.

In this rapt state of moral and intellectual attention to your opponent's inwardness, the ferocity with which you argue your position is in direct proportion to the degree to which you care about it. At the heart of even the most vigorous argument is awe before all the ways to live and before all the obstacles to living. At the end of the most strenuous, intellectually destructive argument is the goal of harmony and wholeness: a stillness.

Stillness, though, has its own impassioned rhetoric, called art.

2

the argument of art

In a fanciful essay about his travels in Italy, the poet Heinrich Heine describes encountering an ancient lizard who is on intimate terms with the stones upon which he likes to take the sun. The lizard explains to the poet that the stones believe God will one day turn himself into a stone so that he will then, the stones say, be able to "save them from their stiffness." Sooner or later, in other words, everyone thinks that even the most dissimilar elements of reality will come to look and think as they do.

By now some readers must want to make the argument that I, having made my living arguing in print, have refashioned reality in the shape of a single, all-encompassing argument.

Just as, so this argument would go, Lenin reduced history to the dynamic of *kto kvo*—who [doing something to] whom—I see argument everywhere, from a newborn's first cries to declarations of love to the ferocious attention to and caring for an aspect of reality that impels me to make a case for or against it. Why, some readers must want to exclaim, he probably finds argument in the way organisms evolve to adapt to their environment! Well, I do in fact see the process of natural adaptation reflected in argument—a good argument adapts to the motion of its counterargument, sometimes even mirroring it. Right now I am making an effort to adapt to a skeptic's arguments the way Darwin's finches grew a particular beak to adapt to their environment's challenges.

Certainly argument as quarrel, dispute, or debate is a specific occasion. But argument in the broadest and deepest sense, as making a case for something, is, as I have tried to show, the way even a neutral-seeming statement holds its own.

I say, this very second, to my wife and children, "I am going to the store." No argument in that. Or is there? In making that statement I have eliminated the possibility of not going to the store. I have to go. If I suddenly decide not to, I must explain why. If I leave and don't go the store, I have to explain why I didn't when I return. If I leave and don't go to the store but come home and say I went, I have to wrestle with the fact that I lied. Even if my conscience is clear, I will be aware of a reality that refutes my original statement that I might someday have to confront.

Overthinking? You'd have to make a case for that, too. Anything new that comes into existence arrives, as Evelyn Underhill put it in *Mysticism,* in the teeth of all arguments. An argument, by definition, seeks to make an abstraction concrete. This makes the reverse also true. Any reality that has sprung into being must make an argument for why it exists. How much do you want for your square?

Now art seems to be an exception. A work of art, whether of literature, the visual arts, or that most abstract art of all, music, transcends the categorical statement that is the mother's milk of argument. Art holds in balanced suspension the conflict and contradiction that would burst into argument in actual life. A novel, a poem, a play, a painting, a sonata, a film, even some popular songs—they are luminous simultaneities of meaning.

To say that a work of art includes an argument is unexceptional. But to define art as an argument seems near-sighted. We think of art as an escape from everyday reality; an escape deeper into reality, to be sure, but an escape nonetheless from the gritty social and psychological factors that thinkers from Aristotle to Kenneth Burke would have us master in order to argue about reality.

An argument has to make its point by means of logic, evidence, and language. Its premises must pass the test of verifiability when they make a logical point and when they make a material point. But what if I write a story that begins with an Iranian woman living in Tehran, who says to her husband and children, "I am going to the store"? That imagined statement fails the test of every requirement for a winning argument. To be accepted as valid, it has first to be accepted as existing. That brings us right back to the ontological nature of argument—and to art.

I rushed into the embrace of art when I was a child, precisely to escape excluding postulates, stinging categoricals, oppressive theses about life. That good, bad, glad, sad, mad Hamlet; helpless, murderous Raskolnikov; Cordelia, so absolutely right and so absolutely wrong; haughty, vulnerable Darcy; monstrous, pathetic Ahab; poor, weak, stupid, heartbreaking Hurstwood—unlike my father's joblessness and later bankruptcy, and my parents' subsequent divorce, the incidents in those characters' lives never stood humiliatingly alone, trapped behind the bars of monotone facts.

I read about situations and personalities, words and gestures that rose up into the imagination on layers of meaning—so many layers that all these overlapping meanings could cushion a guy when he bounced off the hard rock of social reality and started falling. Art imprismed me, you could say, in its extenuating colors, and the multiplicity of truths—of morals to be drawn—set me free.

The basic requirement of any argument is that it be lucid and rational. Art follows a different course. In the realm of language, for example, which is the realm of argument, works of literary art demonstrate the limitations of so-called clear thinking. They present their meanings in patchwork clouds of associations, intuitions, impressions. There are sonnets by Shakespeare that no living person can understand. Their capacity to transfix the reader with their language while hiding their meaning in folds of mind-altering imagery is their rare quality.

Works of literary art are a haven for that part of us that broods over mortal bewilderments, over suffering and death and fleeting happiness. They offer a refuge for our secret self that wishes to contemplate the startling singularity of our physical world, that seeks out the expression of feelings too layered for rational articulation. Literary art's sudden, startling truth and beauty make us feel, in the most solitary part of us, that we are not alone, and that there are meanings that do not decay and die.

It was almost inevitable that the more my passion for the untrammeled freedoms of art intensified, the more that passion led to the essays of Susan Sontag and Lionel Trilling and others, who took on the argument of art in the form of literary arguments about art. For I had discovered that if art proves the existence of an autonomous imagination that is untouched by material pressures, then argument, as a means to expand people's freedom in a particular material situation, is art's complementary dimension. My thirst for one intensified my ardor for the other.

Picasso Was Wrong About Art

The proof that art is an argument lies in the degree to which a work of art gives rise to argument. Keats seemed to intuit this when he wrote the lines at the end of "Ode on a Grecian Urn" that fall on the page with an irrefutable force:

> "Beauty is truth, truth beauty,"—that is all
>   Ye know on earth, and all ye need to know.

The comma after the second "beauty" implies that an apposition will follow, a line that expands on the statement just made. But to expand on meaning is to risk an argument about meaning so Keats cuts himself off with a dash, thus heading off argument. Beauty is truth and truth is beauty because this poem is about truth and beauty, and if this poem, a thing of truth and beauty, identifies truth with beauty, then truth and beauty are identical. It is the most famous circular argument in Western literature.

In Keats's poem, the arguments of art are, simultaneously, about an imaginary situation and about reality. It is an uncanny effect. Keats's ringing declaration—or is it a proclamation?—is a product of the imagination that becomes a fact on the page—"truth beauty": by dropping the verb and fusing subject and predicate, Keats provides material linguistic and typographical proof of the identical meaning of the two words, instead of merely stating it.

Picasso's remark that "art is the lie that discloses the truth" is an elegant piece of romantic nonsense. It is a lie to say that Denmark is in South America. That is a statement that contradicts a provable fact. It is not a lie to tell a story about a young prince who cannot decide whether to exact revenge after his father's ghost tells him that he was murdered by the prince's uncle. A more accurate, if less striking, way to put it would be to say that art is an alternate world that reveals the truth of our familiar world.

Art is not judged by its truth or its validity. The stakes are much higher. Art is judged by the strength of its claims to *be*. Before we agree to judge the truth or validity of a work of art, we have to accept that the world created by a work of art exists.

Years ago, I met a German journalist at a small gathering in the apartment of a mutual friend who was studying modern European literature. We began talking about literature, one thing led to another, and we started to argue about whether Franz Kafka was a comic writer. The German journalist was offended by my suggestion that he was. "You are diminishing the worth of the greatest modern writer in the German language," he said. I argued that Kafka's humor was precisely the measure of his worth.

Fortunately our host had a copy of *The Trial* in English translation and I asked my opponent to consider the novel's famous first sentence: "Someone must have been telling lies about Josef K., he knew he had done nothing wrong but, one morning, he was arrested."

"That's exactly what I mean," the journalist said. "Absolutely chilling." "It does seem that way," I conceded. "But that is not," I said, "how it appeared to Kafka's friends at the time." I recounted how, according to Max Brod, Kafka's best friend and later biographer, Kafka, Brod, and some other friends laughed so hard when Kafka read them the first chapter of *The Trial* that at several points Kafka had to stop his recitation.

The journalist's eyes widened, then he dismissed the point. "Nervous laughter," he replied. "Kafka's evocation of a totalitarian bureaucracy is so frightening that this was the only way they could respond. Plus," he added, "Brod could have fabricated the whole scene because he had his own point to argue, whatever it was."

"Not," I said, "if you look at it from the point of view of Kafka the guilt-ridden Jewish writer and his guilt-ridden Jewish friends. Waking up one morning and getting arrested for no reason must have struck them as something they'd been expecting all their lives."

I realize now that each of us was deploying that old Aristotelian tactic of appealing to authority. As a German, he believed that he possessed the moral urgency necessary to defend the solemn integrity of a great Jewish writer who wrote in his native language. As a Jew, I felt I had to go out on a limb and imply that he, being German, was estranged from Jewish sensibility.

Like the best arguments, the more impassioned ours became, the more it strayed from the calm Apollonian sea of logic and reason toward Dionysian whirlpools of the personal. With so much at stake, far more than we realized, neither of us could convince the other. But it didn't matter. *The Trial* won its argument. Our arguments proved that it existed, that Kafka's surreal novel was as real as saying, "I am going to the store."

Permanently Temporary

Consider, for a moment, that old chestnut of aesthetic theory "the willing suspension of disbelief." Let us say that instead of arguing with advocates of medical rationing, I write a short story about an argument over medical rationing with the aim of advancing my own position on the matter.

In order for such an account to be believed, I would have to water its fictions so that they put down hypothetical roots in reality. I would have to make the characters, their words and gestures, plausible by establishing at every turn a correspondence between my portrait and what is actual. A doctor in favor of medical rationing who suddenly speaks in the demonic language of *The Exorcist* would raise most readers' skeptical eyebrows.

The willing suspension of disbelief that a genuine work of art is supposed to arouse in its audience is based on the degree of correlation between the imagined facts of a work of art and their counterparts in the real world. These run the gamut from the plausible content of a realist novel to the plausible proportions—they must be believably true to the formal proportions they have created—of abstract visual forms and music.

But the truth is that you don't suspend your disbelief in a fictional version of reality unless your most fundamental intuitions about reality are affirmed. You cannot engage in a positive experience like surrendering yourself to a work of art when you are fighting against a negative state of mind. Suspending disbelief in order to accept that a work of art exists is like saying that the foundation of love is the refusal not to love. "How I do not not love you my darling!"

No, the aim of the argument of art is not the willing suspension of disbelief. It is the creation in the audience of what you might call a permanently temporary will to believe. Like Harry Potter on his Quidditch broom, the audience stays aloft on its will to believe only so long as the work of art's plausibility does not tear, a rent in attention that would allow the audience to look down and realize it is defying a natural law by believing the imaginary exists. This will to believe is not the product of a process, as the resolution of an argument is. It happens instantaneously ("once upon a time") or not at all.

At the same time, the creation of a will to believe earns belief in every syllable, every brushstroke, every note. The value of each of these changes even as what they signify comes into view more clearly. A hazy meaning is fatal to the art of argument. A singular clarity is fatal to the argument of art. Is this because despite all our awe-inspiring monuments of reason and morality, life simply happens, life simply *is,* a finality that mocks certainty and exists beyond classification or judgment?

Ashbery's Laugh and Auden's Faithless Arm

When I think of art's supra-rational arguments, I think of meeting the poet John Ashbery at a party and hearing him laugh. Ashbery had become famous for poems whose meanings were infinitely elusive. Their miracle is that they convince readers of their existence not despite their lack of any kind of meaning, but precisely because they lack meaning. Composed out of the weather of everyday life, they prove that climates exist beyond the one we thrive in, climates whose actuality lies in not being consciously understood.

At the time I was working at a magazine where Ashbery occasionally published his poems. An editor at the magazine had told me the following story. As an issue containing one of Ashbery's poems was going through production, someone forgot to remove the sentence "This is dummy copy" (meaning copy that was not to be printed) from the page Ashbery's poem appeared on. Not only that, but the sentence appeared in the magazine as the final line of Ashbery's poem. Yet not a single reader pointed out the error. Apparently Ashbery's poems were so devoid of distinct meaning that they could accommodate any meaning that was tacked on to them.

When I told the story to Ashbery, he neither denied nor confirmed it. He simply threw back his head and roared. The laughter was so clear and strong that I can still hear it. But it did not convey the slightest meaning. In one big bang of risibility, Ashbery had defined the argument of his life's work, which was to reproduce existence in all its unintelligible aliveness.

If, as Shelley claimed, "poets are the unacknowledged legislators of mankind"—as opposed to, say, social media CEOs—then, legislation being the product of argument, argument is the stuff of poetry. Anyway, Yeats's wise and elegant formulation to the contrary, a quarrel is a quarrel, whether with yourself or other people, and in poetry you can see nakedly how art makes its argument that it exists.

> Lay your sleeping head, my love,
> Human on my faithless arm . . .

In "Lullaby," W. H. Auden begins by confessing a lover's infidelity in order to affirm the beauty of "mortal, guilty" humanity. From Catullus to Shakespeare to Christina Rossetti, poets had lamented their lovers' faithlessness. But for Auden in this poem, the power of love has no such bounds, and that boundlessness of love connects it to sympathy and hope.

Yet two verses down, Auden himself is lamenting the fleetingness of "certainty" and "fidelity." He knows very well that the cost to the betrayed is dear. Still, the bursting of conventional bonds is worth it. One night of passion will keep even the betrayed lover "fed by the involuntary powers" of love.

What such lines "mean" is anybody's guess. Infidelity hurts, so why does the poet celebrate it? But customs that bind people to each other despite their failing physical and emotional affinities also hurt, so why not celebrate an escape from them? After all, faithlessness is universal. Then why all the darkness in the poem about infidelity coming with a high cost? Is the pain of betrayal worth the physical delight? Does the inevitability of betrayal really signify "sympathy" and "hope"? Yet does denying the fulfillment of desire that sustains you through, as Auden writes, "noons of dryness" and "nights of insult" make you any happier? What is a dry noon anyway? Is it a reference to Plato's *Phaedrus,* in which "moistness" makes possible the spreading of the lovers' wings in Plato's allegorical conceit? What is a night of insult? Is it when you lie in bed alone, burning with unsatisfied desire? Is it when the beloved turns away from you and goes to sleep?

As the poem's clashing possible meanings appear and vanish, the poem as an original experience becomes more vivid and intense. Your argument about what the poem could mean, with yourself or with someone else, will never be resolved in the form of one categorical statement triumphing over another. You are re-creating, as you read, in your wider and wider embrace of a wholeness filled with contradiction, the prismatic nature of life itself.

Two Sides of Freedom

In the art of argument, the categorical statement that comes after a long line of rhetorical strategies leading up to it is essential. From James Baldwin's "Letter from a Region in My Mind," published in 1962:

> This past, the Negro's past, of rope, fire, torture, castration, infanticide, rape; death and humiliation; fear by day and night, fear as deep as the marrow of the bone; doubt that he was worthy of life, since everyone around him denied it; sorrow for his women, for his kinfolk, for his children, who needed his protection, and whom he could not protect; rage, hatred, and murder, hatred for white men so deep that it often turned against him and his own, and made all love, and trust, all joy impossible—this past, this endless struggle to achieve and reveal and confirm a human identity, human authority, yet contains, for all its horror, something very beautiful.

Baldwin's wrenching sentence arrives toward the end of an essay that has drawn on the Dionysian depths of argument, as Baldwin asserts his authority as a black man, makes use of all that his readers do not know about black experience in America, and tears in the most personal way into the blindness, delusion, and denial that underlie racial prejudice. And he does it in a reinvention of the long periodic sentences that were the hallmark of two pillars of American literature: Henry James and William Faulkner, though Baldwin breaks his periodic sentence apart with a dash—as if he were sundering this convention of a sentence itself with a nod to the long, lilting cadences of the black church, in which his stepfather was a Baptist preacher.

In Baldwin's hands, a semicolon, in the way it builds meaning upon meaning on its path toward a final categorical statement, embodying in this case a chain of suffering that leads to a liberating revelation, is the door to freedom. It is as if in his very grammar Baldwin is arguing for the completion of black existence in America the way a sentence needs a subject and a predicate to be free. In a periodic sentence the predicate comes at the end of a winding journey of clauses. The subject of Baldwin's long sentence is the black experience—"the Negro's past"—and the predicate is stark and simple: "a human identity" that is "something very beautiful." It is an astringent argument to time: an invocation of a slaughterhouse past for the sake of rebuking any future that does not acknowledge and redeem the past. Without that clarity, there is no art of argument.

Allow me to bring in, for the sake of startling contrast, a seemingly wholly unconnected note. It is a passage from a poem, pointedly titled "Poem," by Elizabeth Bishop: "the little that we get for free, / the little of our earthly trust." I could spend a lifetime trying to work through those lines to a categorical statement about the poem in which they appear. At the same time the modest-seeming lines leave on me an unmistakable impression.

What do we ever get "for free" except, perhaps, as the poem movingly proposes, a precious memory—in this case in the form of a poem itself? What does "trust" mean in this context? An inheritance? A faith in something or someone? Both? And if both, what is their relationship to each other?

Yet the lines possess an undefinable distinctness. We know what they mean, beyond being able to explain them, just as we know what to do from one minute to the next without being able to explain why. The uncertainty of stable meaning is a certainty of the freedom of meaning. If we accept that, then not only has the poem won its argument, but we have proven our own autonomy on the evidence of our inwardness. Without the drama of freedom unfolding within us, we can never know how important others' freedom is to them.

The art of argument seeks to make a specific abstraction concrete, from the rights of a woman versus the rights of an unborn child, to the rights of the individual versus the rights of the community, to the virtues of a realist versus an abstract style in painting. You win an argument when you rearrange the given facts. The argument of art, on the other hand, wants simply to be. Rhetoric strives for the vindication of a particular way of living. Art seeks to vindicate the fact of existence itself.

Of course there are occasions when the argument of art becomes an explicit argument itself. So-called novels of ideas, from Voltaire's *Candide* (face life for what it is) to Chinua Achebe's *Things Fall Apart* (pride goeth before even pernicious politics) to Sheila Heti's *How a Person Should Be* (male novelists are too hung up on the hollow pretense of "art"), are arguments for, ultimately, a categorical understanding of the world.

Even novels that seem to have no clear statement about existence sometimes make their creators restless for clarity. Tolstoy appended to the end of *War and Peace* his idiosyncratic theory of history; he attempted to refute G. W. F. Hegel's celebration of world-historical figures by arguing that the higher a figure rises in history, the more that person becomes the plaything of historical forces. And we have all sat through high school or college literature classes in which a work of fiction is wearily reduced to its "theme"—reduced, that is, to yet another argument.

But even the most determined novel, a work of naturalism, say, committed to demonstrating the proposition that human beings are at the mercy of the machinery of society and history, does not press its reductive point unless the author can make it irreducibly alive.

In the hands of the most gifted naturalist writers, this requires only one breathtaking detail. In Richard Wright's *Native Son,* Bigger Thomas and his friends escape the way white society has "blotted" them "out" by going one afternoon to the movie theater. There they try to "blot out" whiteness in turn, in this case by "polishing" their "nightsticks," or masturbating. It is an unforgettable scene in the portrait of Bigger's dehumanization, a stunning revelation of how police brutality has robbed them of their masculinity, replacing the biological instrument of their maleness with the instrument of social enforcement that has robbed them of their maleness.

Unlike the arguments during and around the murder trial that occur at the end of Wright's novel, the scene in the movie theater is irrefutable. It breathes the inarticulable moral atmosphere of life itself.

An Epoch Is an Argument

In its own moment, a historical style of art might seem like a reflection of its circumstances and environment. But artistic style, every bit as much as the dominant style of argument in a given time, is also an argument for a particular way of looking at reality. Naturalism, for example, constitutes a distinct, and polemical, outlook on life.

Years ago, while I was visiting a French friend in Cortona, a small town in Tuscany, she introduced me to Elie Wiesel. An accomplished and also colorful figure, my friend lacked the money to fulfill her dream of adding on a small library to the modest stone farmhouse she owned there. She was at the time trying to persuade both Wiesel and the local Catholic priest to invest in her project, the latter by explaining to him that she wanted to make her library a repository of books about Catholicism, and the former by explaining that she wanted to make her library a repository of books about Judaism. She was a wily, and charming, person.

One sunny afternoon, Wiesel and I took a stroll through Cortona. We began talking about the fate of ancient civilizations. I had taken with me to Italy *Etruscan Places,* one of the three books that D. H. Lawrence wrote about his travels in Italy. Strange and beautiful, the book was also a polemic for the

fascist energy that Lawrence saw all around him and that un-
fortunately he considered a life-affirming alternative to the de-
pression and despair the First World War had induced in the
Italians he met.

Wiesel had not read the book, and he listened graciously
but with sincere interest to my account of Lawrence's description of Etruscan art. Drawing large spiritual conclusions from
Etruscan sculpture, Lawrence argued that Etruscan art embodied everything the Romans lacked: innocence, playfulness,
an openness to wonder rather than a dedication to conquest.
Wiesel nodded and smiled but said nothing.

Inspired by Wiesel, wanting to endear myself to him, I ven-
tured a thought that I had been preoccupied with for weeks. It
could be, I suggested, that seeing they were eventually going to
be crushed by the Romans, the Etruscans destroyed their true
art and left these *tchotchkes*—I used the Yiddish word, meaning a trinket or bauble—lying around so that they could hide
their most beloved secrets from the Romans, and from the
eons of future annihilations. It could be that Lawrence had
been hoodwinked. Wiesel stopped walking. He turned and
laid his hand on my arm. "You have a real feel for lost civilizations," he said softly, without irony.

I feel Wiesel's hand on my arm every time I read a book or
hear a lecture arguing that a historical artistic style is a window

into the intimate thoughts and feelings of the people who lived at that time.

Instead I like to imagine that as Raphael painted a Madonna, some painter down the street from Raphael's studio was breaking reality up into cubes. All the while Shakespeare was constructing his sonnets, another poet was writing in free verse. At the same time that Bach was composing his fugues, someone was creating piano pieces in the style of what would later be Chopin's preludes. But one or another style and its variations came to dominate and exclude all the others.

For this reason it is probably just as accurate to talk about Cinquecento or Elizabethan or baroque works as examples of argument as products of style. They persuade as much as they please. Bach convinces us of order and transcendence; Raphael of compassion as a form of perfection; Shakespeare—as we shall see—of argument as the stuff of life itself. They convince us of these values to the exclusion of other values. They seek to prove the validity of an environment.

Style itself as triumphant argument over competing expressions of truth and beauty may well have been on Milton's mind when he declared, at the end of the first verse of *Paradise Lost,* his purpose in composing the poem:

> That to the highth of this great Argument
> I may assert Eternal Providence,
> And justifie the wayes of God to men.

Alexander Pope's response, made in his "Essay on Man" almost a century later, included an icy dig at his mighty precursor's legendary blindness, declaring his intention to write "of all who blindly creep, or sightless soar"; and to

> Eye Nature's walks, shoot folly as it flies,
> And catch the manners living as they rise;
> Laugh where we must, be candid where we can;
> But vindicate the ways of God to man.

In both cases, the style is an argument that accompanies the content. Milton's unrhymed iambic pentameter had the effect of democratizing, in Protestant eyes, the rigid, authoritarian doctrines of the Catholic Church to the point where a mortal poet named John Milton could speak for both God and Satan. No Catholic poet, even Dante, would have dared that.

Pope's waggish mock-heroic couplets deflate any attempt at religious authority, or transcendence. While Milton seeks to "justify" God's ways to "men," Pope intends to "vindicate" them to "man," as if God had committed transgressions that needed to be defended. His pointed use of "man" instead of Milton's "men" replaces Milton's Calvinist division of the world into saved and damned, Christian and non-Christian, with an Enlightenment ideal of all humans bound by the same values.

Neither poet could have made his argument in the other's style. That would have been like basing a brilliant argument on illogic and lack of evidence.

The Pull of the Familiar

In the fine arts, the argument that each epoch makes for itself is especially dramatic. The very way art history is taught might give the impression that it is as much a study in polemic as in visual representation. You might remember, from Art History 101, the correct answer to that final-exam question about the history of style that got you into Art History 102: Painters like Giotto in the fourteenth century had to make a case against the heavily stylized abstractions of the Middle Ages. Giotto strove to capture the inward thoughts and feelings of his subjects in the representation of their faces. Later painters in Italy picked an argument with Giotto. They felt that his piles of mountains and trees, though more realistic than those of his medieval precursors, failed to depict the physical world's true dimensions. Linear perspective arrived, a development that coincided with an increasing emphasis on humanity over divinity.

Yet both the answer and the question might have missed a larger and more subtle argument.

"The pull of the familiar" is a phrase psychologists sometimes use to describe the fatal gravitational force behind old habits that keep us toiling in the same fruitless patterns of behavior. But one way to look at the history of Western culture is to see the pull of the familiar as the aspiration driving Western art.

Think of the way acting style developed in the West from overblown gestures meant to *signal* an emotion to physical expressiveness meant to *represent* an emotion. Or the way theatrical dialogue, poetic diction, and prose writing have moved closer to the way people actually talk—to the point where reproducing the way people actually talk may have eclipsed the way art used to make sense of the way they actually talk.

It is in the history of painting, however, that art's argument for an ever greater truthfulness to reality is most obvious.

Consider two masterpieces of Dutch art: Jan van Eyck's *Arnolfini and His Bride* (1434) and Johannes Vermeer's *Young Woman with a Water Jug* (1662). Painted over two hundred years apart, the paintings represent two distinct strains of realism; taken together they represent an argument about realism, and about how to perceive the world around us.

Van Eyck's painting is devoid of divinities, saints, or angels. Its two references to holy imagery are represented by possessable things: a statue of a saint at the top of a bedpost and medallions adorning a mirror that portray scenes from the Passion of Christ. The painting is composed of material commodities that can be bought and sold, from the rich velvet bed curtains to the finely wrought chandelier, from the new husband's splendid hat to the lush folds of the bride's gown (you could write the history of Western art over several centuries by following the changing representations of the folds in clothes). But each material thing symbolizes an immaterial verity, from the broom, a token of steady, tidy character, to the single candle burning in the chandelier and the room's reflection in the mirror—allusions to God's all-seeing, all-knowing presence.

Almost as if consciously moving the representation of reality from an intermediate to an advanced level, Vermeer by contrast not only keeps holy figures out of his painting, he strips his possessable material objects of transcendent symbolic value. The water pitcher is just a water pitcher, the window is just a window, and so on. Yet these objects are not common items subject to an ordinary transaction. They are the elements of a person's life captured in the process of becoming the content of a person's unconscious memory. The way the woman's hand grasping the window is seen both on the window and through the window is uncanny. It is a fleeting, unduplicable instant of which she is both the sole possessor and completely unaware.

As for whether she is opening or closing the window, that is a mystery known only to her.

While Van Eck's work is an argument for finding the grace of God in material things, Vermeer's is an argument for the sacredness of every mortal moment on earth, down to the way the map of the Netherlands over the woman's shoulder implies that this rich material geography of a moment is what constitutes a society, a nation. The picture requires no deity to guarantee its right to exist.

Thanks to photography, movies, and digital imaging, we take for granted that the enjoyment of an accurate, even exact representation of visual reality is not a convenience but a right. However, it took centuries for artists to win that right—about as long as it took some societies to arrive at modern notions of justice, fairness, and equality. What people saw every day was not reflected back to them in visual representations of reality.

Imagine going for a horseback ride in Tuscany and savoring the spectacle of hills, trees, and buildings appearing in different sizes behind other hills, trees, and buildings, the distance and scale changing as your horse canters through space, the bells tinkling on the horse's harness as you ride. Afterward you go to church and pass a fresco depicting hills, trees, and buildings piled flatly on top of one another, with no perspective. Walking home you scratch your head and wonder for the umpteenth time why artists can't portray the world the way it really looks.

The right to give the familiar its pull is the argument art has waged since the first cave paintings. It is a perplexity that fire, paper, the wheel, the bow and arrow, methods of irrigation, catapults, and contraceptives were all created long before the architect Filippo Brunelleschi and the painter Masaccio invented linear perspective in the early fifteenth century. It seems that systems of belief had to change before methods of visual representation could evolve. Various prohibitions had to be lifted before one official caste or another would admit that what you saw was the way things actually looked. Galileo had to prove the unseen before painters could accurately portray the seen. First Charles Darwin, then Gustave Courbet.

To make the case for visual reality as people experience it, art has had to push its way through one belief system after another to get to the truth of what is actual. This includes art's evolution into abstraction and conceptualism, both of which seek to represent deeper recesses of emotional and intellectual experience. Mark Rothko said that the solidly realistic goal of his floating abstract rectangles was to make people weep.

The great realist Courbet's remark that "painting is the representation of visible form" is simply the other side of the coin from the great abstractionist Kasimir Malevich's declaration that "a painted surface is a real, living form." Both men were presenting a brief for the essence of painting being its capacity to represent the actual. Piet Mondrian, the purest abstractionist who ever lived, wrote, "It is the task of art to express a clear vision of reality." William Blake, who wrote the argumentative lines "We are led to Believe a Lie / When we see not Thro the Eye," was not just a master of psychological realism in poetry.

He was also a visionary who painted hallucinatory scenes of "truth" that bore no relation to anything visible.

The argument of art has even had to push through the study of art. "To grasp reality," proclaimed the art historian Erwin Panofsky, "we have to detach ourselves from the present." Understanding history, he believed, would make it possible to see how civilizations became what they were. But any understanding of what is dead and gone is a theoretical imposition on the past. Art seeks to grasp the present as an argument for the present, even if it is an argument conducted under the aspect of history.

Art history might well benefit from hewing more closely to immediate psychological realities. The idea, which I referred to above, that the single candle burning in the chandelier and the reflection of the room in the mirror both represent the eye of God is a standard scholarly interpretation of Van Eyck's painting. I'd like to make an alternative argument. Given that Van Eyck wrote in Latin above the mirror, *Johannes de Eyck fuit hic* (Johannes de Eyck was here) the entire painting seems to be arguing for the substitution of the human ego—the possessor of things, the owner of fabulous hats and resplendent gowns— for God himself.

Yet "the pull of the familiar" as an artistic argument is also a paradox. What is familiar—a young woman's water pitcher, for example—acquires an aspect of uniqueness when it is captured in a painting. The familiar seems to pull us most when it is released from the drossy routines of the familiar. A great realist painting shows us the things of the world as they exist when we don't see them. Maybe Elizabeth Murray's three-dimensional painting-sculptures of guitars are how guitars actually look when we are not looking at them. Sometimes a painting is an argument for the majestic autonomy of the ego, as in Van Eyck's Arnolfini painting, and sometimes it is an argument for the irrelevancy of our self-importance.

There should be some sort of doctrine of the familiar since a work of visual art's inclusion of a familiar detail, whether it is an embroidered slipper in a rendition of the Madonna and Child or a horse's ear in one of Susan Rothenberg's idiosyncratic, semi-abstract depictions of a horse, is art's version of driving home an argument with a piece of evidence.

All great arguments rely on the prop of a familiar detail. Movies use props to make their case all the time. Would we be as convinced of Marlon Brando's conversion from heartless thug to angel of rescue in *On the Waterfront* if, in the character of a former boxer, he had not in an unscripted moment absent-mindedly slipped his hand into Eva Marie Saint's glove as he stood talking with her in a park, thus revealing his sympathetic feminine side? Would Dionne Warwick's song have been on every working girl's lips if she had not included the details of an ordinary day: "While combing my hair now / And wondering what dress to wear now." Bruce Springsteen made an argument along similar lines, as he constructed a case for highways "jammed with broken heroes": "Girls comb their hair in rear-view mirrors, and the boys try to look so hard." The familiar objects of comb, hair, mirror, suspended in time and space, clinch the argument that these songs exist as an original experience in the listener's mind.

Prosecutors will clutch a journal that belonged to the murder victim as they make the summation to the jury; a defense lawyer will hold up a toy bear that belongs to the daughter of the alleged murderer. Orators cherish the familiar detail. In his speech to the Democratic National Convention in 2020, Barack Obama artfully used the words "train," "last one in the room," "next semester's classes," "city centers," "airports," "rural roads." Donald Trump relied on familiar schoolyard insults to some of the country's most elevated figures in order to throw them under the populist wave that was sweeping the country. I have used personal anecdotes to try to lure you into vicariously inhabiting my arguments—and though the bells tinkling on the horse's harness on my hypothetical ride through Tuscany might be an alien image, everyone knows the sound of bells tinkling.

The Role of Feeling

The literary artist whose achievement represents the pinnacle of the artistic imagination is also the figure who plumbed the depths of the familiar by illuminating the cracks, niches, and crevices of ordinary life. In a single play, Shakespeare is able to portray every stratum of society and every inflection of consciousness in language that extends from the colloquial to the eloquent to the sublime. You find, as it were, Dionne Warwick and Piet Mondrian not just in the same play but in the same scene.

But what is most striking, as the several occasions on which I've already quoted from Shakespeare's plays reflect, is that Shakespeare's language, resonating in all its strangeness with the familiar patterns of existence, always settles into argument.

Start with the sonnets. Choose a sonnet by Shakespeare at random, and you will find an argument. From its inception in Italy, the sonnet had always had an argument at its heart, but the reinvention of the sonnet in English in the early 1500s made argument its inevitable form. Shakespeare brought the sonnet as argument to the peak of perfection. Even the most famous and seemingly most simple of his sonnets has a polemical intent:

> Shall I compare thee to a summer's day?
> Thou art more lovely and more temperate:

Rough winds do shake the darling buds of May,
And summer's lease hath all too short a date:
Sometime too hot the eye of heaven shines,
And often is his gold complexion dimmed,
And every fair from fair sometime declines,
By chance, or nature's changing course untrimmed:
But thy eternal summer shall not fade,
Nor lose possession of that fair thou ow'st,
Nor shall death brag thou wander'st in his shade,
When in eternal lines to time thou grow'st,
   So long as men can breathe, or eyes can see,
   So long lives this, and this gives life to thee.

The thesis is plain. The poet is telling the object of his love, a young man, that although the young man's exceptional physical beauty will fade as all human beauty fades, his radiant youth will live on in the immortal lines of the poem he is reading.

This is a fairly arrogant argument to make, and the poet knows it. But instead of ironically acknowledging his presumption, he becomes even more brazen in pressing his case. Shall I compare you to a summer's day? Well you're even more lovely and more gentle than a summer's day, but when you think about it, that's not really saying much since summer can get pretty ugly, what with winds blowing everything all over the place and the heat and humidity. Let's drop the summer simile then and state the unlovely truth: beautiful forms decline, and even the most remarkable of them become plain in time. So listen, my dear, your only hope of beating the ravages of aging is having me sing your praises in my poetry, and if you think that sounds like an attractive exchange, then why don't you come by the theater tonight after everyone has gone home and we'll talk about it?

In the plays of Shakespeare, poetic language becomes argument the way pistil and stamen grow into a flower.

Hamlet argues with his mother, Kate argues with Petruchio, Oberon argues with Titiana, *Romeo and Juliet* opens with two servants quarreling about quarreling, to take only a few examples. Perhaps language at its most liberated and its most expressive bends toward argument just as surely as "the arc of the moral universe" was said to "bend toward justice," in another famous argument.

Full-bodied argument, often in the form of a trial, appears as a significant scene or watershed moment in one play after another. *The Merchant of Venice* turns on a trial near the end of the play. Mark Antony in *Julius Caesar* nimbly whips the mob up against Brutus and Cassius in a kind of trial. *King Lear* begins with language twisted into a fatal rhetoric by vanity and greed and reaches its devastating conclusion partly by means of, appropriately, a travesty of a trial. In *Henry IV, Part I,* a mock trial, in which Falstaff impersonates the king, provides comic relief. In *A Winter's Tale,* Leontes puts his wife on trial and serves as judge. *Measure for Measure* depicts a world where the law and appetite collide, producing crashing moral perspectives, a world where justice is transactional and threats, ultimatums, and pleas take the place of arguments. In *Othello,* Iago persuades Roderigo that Desdemona is in love with Cassio in an extraordinary argument composed of insinuation, manipulative imperatives—argument from authority—and circular reasoning. (Iago, one of the most formidable arguers in the history of literature, perhaps recalled Aristotle's guide to psychology the instant he sensed that Othello's fragile sense of self was reflected in his overblown flights of language: "Oh, beware, my lord, of jealousy . . .").

Only *Troilus and Cressida,* though, explores the very nature of argument, as if in that play Shakespeare were taking stock of his artistic obsession. Said to have been written for an audience of lawyers, the play examines opinion as the basis of knowledge, and scrutinizes shifting notions of value as the basis of opinion—"Men prize the thing ungained more than it is," says Cressida (i.e., by seeming unattainable, things are valued more than they are worth).

Along with fools and mad kings, Shakespeare often put wisdom in the mouths of his most unsavory characters—"Simply the thing I am shall make me live" says Parolles in *All's Well That Ends Well,* a surprisingly honest appraisal from this cowardly, deceitful character of his nature and his limitations. From the time of the *Iliad,* the outrageously overbearing figure of Thersites has played the role of foul-mouthed, apoplectic truthteller. In *Troilus and Cressida,* to expose the roots of argument, Shakespeare develops this stock character to his fullest human extent. Commenting on the argument between Agamemnon and Achilles over Achilles' slave girl, Thersites cries:

> Here is such patchery, such juggling and such
> knavery! all the argument is a cuckold and a
> whore; a good quarrel to draw emulous factions
> and bleed to death upon. Now, the dry serpigo on
> the subject! and war and lechery confound all! (3.2.70–74)

Thersites refers to the emotions that manipulate perceptions of reality—"such patchery, such juggling"—as the engine behind argument. He reduces argument to its origins, both dark and mundane, in everyday clashes of ego and desire (argument is a "cuckold" and a "whore"), and also to plain old rivalry and envy ("emulous factions"), ending in a conflagration of "war" and "lechery," lechery in this sense most likely signifying the atrocity of rape that accompanies war. This is the fate of argument in a world that has reduced all meaning to questions of power. It is Kenneth Burke's worst nightmare.

Leave aside Thersites' vision of social chaos. Thersites is stating in street talk one of the play's central propositions about the mechanism that causes argument, and shapes argument. Wrong opinion is often the product of bias, and bias is the outcome of strong emotion. The value we put on a person or thing is not some objective, measurable value. Its value consists in the value we impose on it. Thus the importance of emotion in argument. It can confer on a weak argument the value of a strong one. That is why there is often a thin line between a convincing argument and a seductive one.

Lawyers instinctively know this; it is why criminal lawyers sometimes go to acting coaches to learn how to conduct a case before judge and jury. Arguing a case is not easy: the judge enforces calm; a jury can be moved by the right amount of feeling. Of course manipulative testimony dispassionately orchestrated can have the same effect as a lawyer who breaks down during his summation. Editorial writers know the value of a display of feeling. They use emotional language when pressing a point of arid policy that will nevertheless have a great effect and try to appear dry and rational when explicitly appealing to the emotions.

The deployment of artifice is as important to an argument as the force of reason. The audience may decide how far out on a limb an arguer may go, but the arguer has to determine to what extent to let the audience into the secret of the performance; by sharing with the audience a winking acknowledgment that he or she is acting, the arguer may persuade the audience to accept greater displays of emotion. These might well have the effect, despite the audience's awareness of the artifice, of sweeping the listeners into genuine passion. "You cannot both be sincere and act sincere," said André Gide. An arguer has to judge the occasion and the audience to decide when the right time is for each.

Of course everything depends on whether an argument is made for a person reading in solitude or for an assembled group seated before the speaker or the television, a medium that exaggerates the slightest physical gesture into grotesque excess. "The camera likes emptiness," Norman Mailer once wrote. Make an argument before the camera in short, simple sentences, and you will flatter it into thinking you have nothing to say that cannot be captured by the lens. Use a subordinate clause just once, and you make the camera feel inferior. It goes to sleep.

The movie or the television camera, a piece of technology far removed from nature, ironically hates artificiality. It adores pure, animal-like unself-consciousness. Just as all art aspires to the condition of music (as someone once said), acting grows naturally into an argument for plausibility—"Yes, that is how someone would behave in that situation!"—a plausibility made convincing by the force of pure physicality. This is why the camera found in Marilyn Monroe the natural release it needed. Kennedy demolished Nixon in the first televised presidential debate because he had as profound an affinity with the camera as Monroe did. The camera embraced their arguments—perhaps it also helped them make each other's acquaintance.

This brings us back to popular art, and to acting. An argument always offers a good amount of entertainment. Entertainment always offers a fair amount of argument. And the essence of entertainment is pleasurable, or releasing, emotion.

"There was a disturbance in my heart, a voice that spoke there and said, *I want, I want, I want!* It happened every afternoon, and when I tried to suppress it, it got even stronger." Saul Bellow put these words in the mouth of Eugene Henderson, his middle-aged Huckleberry Finn, but if popular art had a manifesto, this would nicely sum it up. Popular art is about "I want" in all its infinite forms, mutations, fluctuations in a human existence. And "I want" is the essence of argument. Indeed, as we alluded to earlier, Method acting requires actors to ask themselves three fundamental questions before beginning the process of inhabiting a character: "What do I want?" "Why do I want it?" "How will I get it?" Those are not bad questions to ask about yourself, and your opponent, before you begin to construct an argument.

Satire, as we have seen with Swift, makes its counterargument simply by a holding a gimlet-eyed mirror up to the original argument. Published in 1948 by the British humorist Paul Jennings, "Report on Resistentialism" is a scathingly funny rebuttal, by a devoutly Catholic writer, of the French existentialism that was overtaking Western thought. In the course of its witty devastations, it makes a powerful point about the fate of wanting.

Against Jean-Paul Sartre's assertion that "Man is nothing else than what he makes of himself," Jennings posited the intransigence of inanimate things, which thwart "man" at every turn. Resistentialism's motto is *Les chose sont contre nous*—"things are against us": it "offers us a grand vision of the Universe as One Thing—the Ultimate Thing (*Dernière Chose*). And it is against us." Pianos, medicine cabinets, "the way honey gets between the fingers," and a scientific experiment conclusively proving that when a piece of toast with marmalade is dropped on a cheap carpet, it always falls with the marmalade right side up, while when it is dropped onto priceless Chinese silk, it always falls face down—these all prove the futility of human beings' struggle with the inanimate world.

The essay is delightful as it builds from absurdity about existentialist absurdity to absurdity, but it possesses an unfunny truth about the intransigence of mortal conditions. Not only do you not get everything you want, but when you do, it is always at the expense of something else you want; and once you get it, it doesn't last. Virgil phrased our earthly conundrum more somberly but was presenting a similar idea when he wrote in the *Aeneid* of *rerum lacrimae,* the "tears in things." He meant "things" in the broad, Latin sense of pretty much anything. And in that sense, "things" are ultimately intractable. They make an argument with them a permanent condition of everyday life.

Words and Music

In high art, as we have seen, official versions of reality had to evolve before art could more accurately portray what people experienced. Popular art, rooted in experience, follows a similar trajectory, but a more accelerated one. The pictures of experience presented by popular art are being continuously reconfigured as one socially dominant version of reality gives way to another.

A rising backlash to the 1990 movie *Home Alone,* for example, sometimes using expert testimony from medical doctors, makes the argument that the sensationally violent film is, as the Associated Press put it, "an insidious gateway drug, acclimating children the world over to the next level of related thrills and methodical kills found in the slasher genre."

Perhaps not, but in any case, the movie presents the traditional argument of fairy tales and children's stories. Nearly all of them, from the Grimm Brothers to the *Harry Potter* series, portray orphanhood as a child's worst conscious fear and deepest unconscious desire. It is an argument that makes even the most sophisticated people feel uncomfortable. After hiring Oscar Wilde as a babysitter, Yeats and his wife arrived home to find their children sobbing in fright. It seems that at bedtime Wilde had read to the children one of his own fairy tales, themselves arguments against conventional taste. He was immediately dismissed.

The locus classicus, currently, of how social perceptions radically alter the value of a work of popular art is the song "Baby, It's Cold Outside." The holiday classic has gone from being seen as a playfully seductive plea in the tradition of Andrew Marvell's "To His Coy Mistress" (amid the rising snows in the blizzard of mortality, let's make love, and fast) to a veiled apology for date rape. Too often, though, the origins of the song, and its many different versions, go unacknowledged in the debate.

The song probably did not enter dangerous waters until 1959, when a louche Dean Martin crooned it with shameless self-assurance to a female chorus representing the helpless Eternal Feminine. Before that, to take just one of its many versions,

Louis Armstrong and Velma Middleton sang the seductive song together as a joke about the seductive song. Armstrong: "Look-a there honey . . . look at that window there . . . you can't go out there in all that bad weather take a look . . . you lookin' at the wrong window anyway . . . that's a bay window there . . . See the one that's in the middle there . . . yeah the one that's boarded up . . . that's an outhouse there . . ."

In the film where the song originally appeared, *Neptune's Daughter,* Ricardo Montalban first tries to seduce Esther Williams as they sing it, then Betty Garrett and Red Skelton sing it again later in the movie with the tables reversed, as Garrett tries to convince Skelton to stay the night.

Nevertheless, the song, which once embodied a transparent argument about sex, has now been moved to the center of a larger argument about power—just as the art of argument itself is now often submerged in a larger argument about power. In that sense, the song has been successful beyond the most excited ambitions of its composer, Frank Loesser, who used to sing it with his wife as the closing number of their nightclub act when they wanted the audience to know that it was time to go home. Today the audience would stay and argue.

Songs are only one form of musical argument. Ancient societies did not use poetry or painting to rouse soldiers to battle;

they employed music. As the most subjective of the arts, music has the most direct and immediate emotional effect, and it causes the most impassioned arguments. Perhaps turning a piece of music into a matter of contention serves the purpose of putting pure feeling under intellectual control.

It might seem absurd to say that a form of music like the waltz made anything resembling an argument. But a style of dance in which the partners held each other more closely than polite society had ever allowed gave rise to heated debate. The question of whether the waltz itself presented an argument becomes—almost—moot. Anything new is an argument against what it suddenly defines as old. In the case of music, its status as the most abstract of the arts makes it, paradoxically, the most open to the imposition on it of debatable categorical statements.

This can be said for every type of popular music. The blues became controversial when it opened the door to women singers declaring their independence and expressing their sexuality in a way unknown before. Here an argument was being made in particular to a society that argued back in general. Swing, bebop, cool jazz, Sinatra, the Beatles, every sort of rock, hip hop—in a sense, music reproduces in every age the argument between the Furies and Athena in Aeschylus's *Eumenides:* To what degree can society allow itself to be influenced either by feeling or by thought? No wonder some people believed that Elvis's gyrations were the beginning of Western civilization's downward spiral.

The most recent argument provoked by musical form was over hip hop and rap. Hip hop's practitioners themselves often define the style as, above all, a style of argument. Ahmir "Questlove" Thompson wrote that "the greatest hip-hop songs have the power to pull energy and excitement and anger and questions and self-doubt and raw emotion out of you. . . . The common thread is change. The best hip-hop songs aren't blueprints—they are calls to action, reminders that you can start a revolution in three minutes." Of course one person's call to action is another person's defense of the status quo, and as we have seen, the fundamental form of argument often comes down to a struggle between looking to the past and looking to the future. Replying to hip hop's defenders, the jazz critic Stanley Crouch argued that hip hop was another form of minstrelsy, a distorted presentation of white stereotypes of black life as violent and nihilistic, created by and for greedy white music producers: "Narcissism and anarchic resentment are promoted in such a calculated fashion that numbskull pop stars pretend to be rebels while adhering to the most obvious trends. . . . These people are not about breaking taboos, they are about making money."

Perhaps there is a moment, "once in a lifetime," as Seamus Heaney wrote, when "hope and history rhyme," and perhaps one could argue that those lines are somewhat grandiose, since they can be true only if in that exceptional moment hope and history rhyme for all the good people who are caught up in it, but someone is always left out. What is certain is that sometimes popular art matches the rhythm, if not the rhyme, of history. American rap and the argument about race it dramatizes offers one example. So does Pierre Beaumarchais's *Le Mariage de Figaro* as a catalyst for the French Revolution, jazz as a declaration of freedom by the Solidarity movement in Poland, and Tunisian hip hop as a rallying cry in the months leading up to the ill-fated Arab Spring. All these musical instances sought to make an abstract truth concrete.

Arguments in the Key of Life

In J. D. Salinger's "Seymour: An Introduction" a prominent music critic becomes annoyed with his daughter's public school when he learns that as a member of the Glee Club she and the other children are being taught to sing popular songs by the likes of Harold Arlen, Jerome Kern, and Irving Berlin. The children should, he huffs to himself, be singing "simple little Schubert Lieder instead of that 'trash.' " So off he goes to the principal to complain about the music teacher. Impressed by the "arguments," as Salinger puts it, of such an eminent figure, the principal agrees to admonish the teacher. Smugly content with his triumph over vulgar, popular taste, the music critic leaves the school, walking with a spring in his step down the street as he whistles "K-K-K-Katy."

The irony goes beyond the obvious hypocrisy of the high-minded critic diverting himself with a popular song after his defense of high art. "K-K-K-Katy" is about a young soldier named Jimmy, afflicted with a devastating stutter, who courts, then marries a young woman before he goes off to fight in the First World War, probably to be killed, almost certainly to be maimed in some way. It is about, in other words, an experience that is as sorrowful as the most sorrowful of Schubert's songs.

The critic whistling a song with such painful meaning makes him complicit in the trivializing of profound experience that he seems to decry in popular music. But this is where the irony comes to an end. The complicated question that haunts this incident is the role of art, and of popular art, and of the relationship between them, and between them and life. Each definition, in each category, is an argument.

The fact that the song enters the critic's mind spontaneously and naturally, behind his conscious, rational will, makes the case that popular art has its sources in the wellsprings of life every bit as much as high art does. Yet the song itself is also an argument against its own genre. For there are actually two songs. One is the song that tells the story of Jimmy and Katy. The other is the song that Jimmy sings to Katy within that song. That song, the one Jimmy sings, goes like this:

> "K-K-K-Katy, beautiful Katy,
> You're the only g-g-g-girl that I adore;
> When the m-m-m-moon shines,
> Over the cow shed,
> I'll be waiting at the k-k-k-kitchen door."

The larger song comments on Jimmy's song:

> Now he's off to France the foe to meet.
> Jimmy thought he'd like to take a chance,
> See if he could make the Kaiser dance,
> Stepping to a tune,
> All about the silv'ry moon,
> This is what they hear in far off France.

In other words, "K-K-K-Katy" is really a cynical tune about a young man who sings a starry-eyed tune, unaware of the pain and heartbreak that loom over him and his girl, even projecting his buoyancy onto the Kaiser, believing that he can make his powerful adversary "dance" under a "silv'ry moon." And the critic, for all his cultural sophistication, is just as unaware as Jimmy of the simultaneous meanings of the song. Is he whistling romantic, hopeful Jimmy's deluded melody, or the larger song's cynical, yet wholly aware, one? Both at once, no doubt, just as Jimmy is at the same time "brave and bold" and doomed to trauma, injury, or death. The critic's young daughter, whether she learns Schubert or "K-K-K-Katy," will sooner or later find herself in the same web of mystery and mortality. No one escapes the imprisoned meanings of human existence. In the same way that the women, mortal and divine, whom Odysseus meets on his journey home are all dream-forms of Penelope, the critic ends up being an incarnation of Jimmy, who is an incarnation of Seymour, who returned from the First World War traumatized before taking his own life.

It is Seymour, after all, who relates the story of the music critic to his brother Buddy—the narrator of "Seymour"—as a response to a story that Buddy has written and has just read aloud to him. Buddy's story, Seymour says, rises above its own sentimentality, and Seymour wishes that, in this respect, Buddy had "slipped up a little" and given sentimentality its due. So Seymour tells this story about the critic, and Jimmy, and the sentimental song that is as true to reality as Schubert's lieder. And Buddy includes Seymour's story in the story he is now writing about Seymour, a story that is as defiantly sentimental as it is unabashedly sophisticated, just as Jimmy sings his song in another song, which is a sentimental song that turns on its own sentimentality while remaining sentimental . . . Life, and art, and popular art, and the contentions between them, go on and on and on.

epilogue

The current American moment, roiling with clashing opinions and beliefs about the most fundamental realities, operates like a grinding of geological plates in the process of reconfiguring a part of the earth. By now, the lamentably frequent complaint has become almost moribund in its familiarity: the country seems to have disappeared down the proverbial rabbit hole where what used to be known as facts are now considered either matters of opinion or products of ideology.

To return for a minute to Shakespeare's *Troilus and Cressida:* as Troilus puts it, "What is aught, but as 'tis valued?" Value is strictly a matter, he is arguing, of, as we would say, optics. If enough people put value on something, then regardless of its intrinsic worth, it has value. The play is full of what literary critics call "rhetorical redescription." This is a rhetorical gambit in which something morally repugnant is forcefully represented as being morally attractive. In such a world, perjury is no more than a rhetorical strategy, and language becomes, as Troilus says, "words, words, mere words." If that world were to materialize, then

> . . . right and wrong,
> Between whose endless jar justice resides,
> Should lose their names, and so should justice too.
> Then every thing includes itself in power. (1.3.119–122)

The nightmare menace of a world in which reality has become subjective leads to a dissolution of language, which then leads to a world defined by naked imbalances of power—a world in which argument becomes impossible.

Or has argument simply taken a new turn?

Argument, as a process bound up with our very right to exist, has always occupied its crucial space at the heart of a paradox: the raw imbalance of power that makes argument impossible is also the source of the eternal necessity of argument. Only argument can redress an imbalance of power without setting in motion an endless cycle of revenge. "The strong do what they can and the weak suffer what they must," the militarily superior Athenians, in 416 BCE, tell the Melian delegation that has come to beg for mercy for their besieged city. In a situation where this is true, argument dies; yet in such a situation, argument becomes identified with freedom itself.

Endless debate between whites, between whites and blacks, and between blacks led to an impasse in which actions causing reactions were all that could move civil rights forward in the United States. The violence that Martin Luther King's policy of nonviolence unleashed—or exposed—culminating in the murder of the three Freedom Riders in Mississippi in June 1964, led to the signing of the Civil Rights Act one month later. That, in turn, led to another long stretch of argument about just how and to what degree the process of securing civil rights should proceed, an argument that now, it seems, has brought us to the impasse of action and reaction in the realm of culture at which the Black Lives Matter movement appears to have found itself. The conflict between retributive passion and rational justice, as contentious today as in the debate between the Furies and Athena in the *Eumenides,* never ends. In that ceaseless seesaw motion, argument is sometimes the midwife of an epoch in which argument cannot find a place.

Perhaps in the cycle of argument, history, argument, we are now at such a place, a place where only power can redress an imbalance of power: "Will you shut up, man?" a seemingly exasperated Joe Biden snapped at Donald Trump during their first presidential debate. If this happens, then until the cycle revolves into a cooler phase, every intellectual opponent will be an "It," not a "Thou," and what distinguishes a potent argument will not be a mental appeal to the emotions but a tremendous emotional spur to action. In such a moment, vicarious introspection yields to the belief that the position of the other side is detrimental to a common humanity.

Or perhaps we are at the dawn of new arguments in a different idiom: the realm of art, for example, where one case or another has always been made for the precious relationship between human inwardness and human freedom:

Eternal Spirit of the chainless Mind!
(George Gordon, Lord Byron, "Sonnet on Chillon")

The question of whether argument is still possible might, for now, be the most urgent argument we can have.

Most of the references and quotations in this book are drawn from classic works and thus easily accessible: Aristotle's *Rhetoric,* translated by Robin Waterfield; Plato's *Lysis* and *Gorgias* (which contains the comparison of argument to cooking), in Benjamin Jowett's translation; Thucydides' *History of the Peloponnesian War,* translated by Rex Warner (which includes Pericles' Funeral Oration and the story of the Melian ambassadors).

A few works, however, have illuminated my thinking despite themselves being undeservedly obscure, and a few, because they have become deservedly renowned, have become disconnected from their actuality as texts.

The Character of Logic in India, by Bimal Krishna Matilal, the late Indian philosopher, introduced me to a basic taxonomy of argument in Hindu thought, while the Qur'an provided me with the Prophet's reflections on the usefulness of debate. (Suras 6 and 40 are especially instructive in the psychological stratagems of argument.) The sharp exchange between Buddha and the Brahmin Assayalana can be found in *The Middle Length Discourses of the Buddha: A New Translation of the Majjhima Nikāya,* translated by Bhikkhu Ñāṇamoli and Bhikkhu Bodhi (1995). Unless otherwise indicated, biblical quotations are from the New International Version.

Heinz Kohut's original formulation of empathy as "vicarious introspection" appears in Kohut's seminal paper "Introspection, Empathy, and Psychoanalysis," published in the *Journal of the American Psychoanalytical Association* in 1959.

For many years, I believed that the aphorism "When you meet a contradiction, make a distinction" originated with Thomas Aquinas, an error that might have been the result of reading, when I was in my twenties, William James's essay "What Pragmatism Means" (1907), in which he identifies the idea as a "scholastic adage," an attribution that over the years I mentally misfiled under "Aquinas." I cannot find the quotation, which makes me suspect that James might have misfiled it after coming up with it himself. Whatever its origin, it's a great line.

Stephen Vincent Benet's marvelously fanciful story "The Devil and Daniel Webster" was once, as I note, a staple of the American high school curriculum, but it has now gone the way of, well, the American high school curriculum. It can be found in numerous collections of Benet's work. Thomas Kuhn's concept of "paradigm shifts" appears in his once widely cited *The Structures of Scientific Revolutions,* published in 1962.

Montaigne's earthy scatological deflation of kings and philosophers occurs in his essay "On Experience." It seems appropriate to mention, along those lines, that Joan Didion's laconic response to a lengthy letter that criticized a piece by her appeared in the October 11, 1979, issue of the *New York Review of Books.*

F. Scott Fitzgerald's definition of a "first-rate intelligence" can be found in his volume of essays *The Crack-Up* (1945), edited by Edmund Wilson.

Mussolini's "Speech to the People of Rome" has been collected in the now out-of-print *Readings in Western Civilization,* edited by George Knoles and Rixford K. Snyder. The best edition of Cicero's so-called Catilinarians—his celebrated speeches condemning the aristocratic Roman conspirator Catiline—is Oxford University Press's *Cicero's Catilinarians,* edited by D. H. Berry (2020). Cicero's advice about abusing the plaintiff occurs in his *Pro Flacco,* rendered into English by C. Macdonald. My quotations from his *De oratore* are from the 1988 edition of that work, translated by E. W. Sutton and H. Rackham.

The Lionel Trilling quotations are from Trilling's introduction to his 1950 *The Liberal Imagination*. Reinhold Niebuhr's reflections on irony can be found in his 1952 *The Irony of American History*. Happily, for all their density and abstruseness, Kenneth Burke's *Grammar of Motives* (1945) and his *Rhetoric of Motives* (1950) are still in print, thanks to the good graces of the University of California Press. Anyone interested in exploring Method acting's notions of "wanting" in acting should start with Stella Adler's *The Art of Acting* (2000) and Richard Boleslavsky's *Acting: The First Six Lessons* (1949); Foster Hirsch's history of the Method, *A Method to Their Madness* (1984), is a helpful guide.

My quotations from James Baldwin can be found in his long essay "Letter from a Region in My Mind," first published in 1962 in the *New Yorker*. Martin Luther King's statement of disillusionment with white liberals is from an essay that he published in the *Saturday Review* in 1965. Norman Mailer made his observations on the camera in *Advertisements for Myself* (1959). Heinrich Heine's fanciful tale about the talking lizard appears in his *Travel Pictures* (1826). Picasso's mot about art and truth is quoted by Alfred Barr in *Picasso: Fifty Years of His Art* (1946). Max Brod's anecdote about Kafka reading to his friends from *The Trial* appears in Brod's biography of Kafka (1937), translated by G. Humphreys-Roberts and Richard Winston (1960).

The quotation from William Blake is from *The Complete Poetry and Prose of William Blake,* edited by David Erdman (1982). Yeats's elegant formulation about quarrel can be found in his *Per Amica Silentia Lunae.* Péguy's remark about mystery and politics appears in his *Notre Jeunesse,* and Gide made his mot about sincerity in his *Journals,* translated by Justin O'Brien (1987). Martin Buber's *I and Thou* exists in a fine translation by Walter Kaufmann (1971). Seamus Heaney's over-quoted line about hope and history is from his *The Cure at Troy: A Version of Sophocles' Philoctetes* (1991).

In the sections on the visual arts, I drew my quotations from Gerstle Mack's *Courbet* (1951); Kasimir Malevich's "From Cubism and Futurism to Suprematism" (1915); Philip B. Meggs's 1983 *History of Graphic Design* (where the reader can find the quotation from Mondrian); and Erwin Panofsky's *Meaning in the Visual Arts: Papers in and on Art History* (1955).

The phrase "willing suspension of disbelief" is bruited about so casually it might be worthwhile to observe that it belongs to Samuel Taylor Coleridge, who wrote in chapter 14 of his *Biographia Literaria* (1817) that such an imaginative capacity "constitutes poetic faith" itself.

Paul Jennings's satirical piece "Report on Resistentialism" was collected by Dwight Macdonald in his *Parodies: An Anthology from Chaucer to Beerbohm—and After* (1960). Sartre's counter-assertion can be found in "Existentialism and Human Emotions" (1985) translated by Bernard Frechtman and Hazel E. Barnes. The quote from Saul Bellow is from *Henderson the Rain King* (1959).

Ahmir "Questlove" Thompson's description of hip-hop was published in *Rolling Stone* in December 2012. The quote about rap music from the late, profoundly missed Stanley Crouch appeared in the June 12, 1995, issue of *Time* magazine.

Finally, whatever I have come to understand about Shakespeare's infinitely complex *Troilus and Cressida* I learned from the magnificent Frank Kermode, whose lectures on Shakespeare I had the precious good fortune to attend as a graduate student at Columbia.

Lee Siegel, the celebrated author of seven books and a recipient of the National Magazine Award for Reviews and Criticism, publishes widely on culture and politics. He lives with his wife and their two children in Montclair, New Jersey.

Featuring intriguing pairings of authors and subjects, each volume in the Why X Matters series presents a concise argument for the continuing relevance of an important idea.

Also in the series